THE DYNAMITE KIDS' GUIDE TO THE MOVIES

by Margaret Ronan

Illustrations by Montxo Algora

A Dynamite Book from Scholastic Paperbacks

This book is for movie fans —
and you know who you are!

The Book You Are Holding Is 100% Dynamite!

Yes, Dynamite Books come to you from the same
scintillating scribblers and peerless pen-and-inkers who
bring you Dynamite Magazine every month: Jane Stine,
Series Editor; Greg Wozney Design, Art Direction;
Sharon Graham and Judy Gorman, Production
Editors; Susan Hood, Assistant Editor; and the
whole Hot Stuff gang!

Cover Illustration/Montxo Algora

ISBN: 0-590-31228-6

12 11 10 9 8 7 6 5 4 3 2 1   5   0 1 2 3 4 5/8

Printed in the U.S.A.   08

COMING ATTRACTIONS

Would You Believe?

Buster Keaton eyes a pie.

Remember the scene in *The Wizard of Oz* where Judy Garland sings, "Somewhere Over the Rainbow"? Would you believe Louis B. Mayer, the head of MGM Studios, wanted that scene cut out of the movie. He said it was "boring."

Remember B movies? They were low-budget quickies, made for the lower half of double bills. Republic Studios made nothing but B's. Screenwriters at Republic never got to go to story conferences. Herbert Yates, Republic's boss, would send them a title to build a screenplay around. Sometimes they only got three days to do the job. Some Yates titles: *Prison Nurse; Red River Renegades; Danger, Women at Work; Mystery Broadcast; Lake Placid Serenade.* If you can think up a story to go with those titles, maybe you belong in Hollywood.

Throwing custard pies at people looks easy, but comic Buster Keaton took it seriously. In his 1939 movie *Hollywood Cavalcade,* he was supposed to hit Alice Faye in the face with a pie from a distance of six feet. Keaton made a practice pie out of wood with nails sticking out of it. Then he threw it over and over at an outline of Alice on the wall. The practice paid off. When the cameras rolled, the scene took only one (custard) pie and one take.

If you think Hollywood stars work hard, picture this. In India, stars work in three or four (or even more) movies at the same time. It's not unusual for an Indian actor to race from soundstage to soundstage, muttering lines from one movie while rushing to do a scene for another. Luckily the directors aren't too fussy. One take is usually enough.

Bob Hope eyes Dorothy Lamour.

In the 1930's, a man named John Lovell invented the "smellies" — a machine that flooded movie theaters with different smells to match the action on the screen. It didn't catch on. Aren't you glad?

Do you ever wonder if the food you see in movies is real? Some of it is, but false food is used in many eating scenes. Whipped cream is made of shaving cream, lettuce and pickles are made of rubber, and those fresh fruits and vegetables often turn out to be fresh plastic. For reasons too easy to guess, real alcohol is never used in drinking scenes. Plain cold tea doubles for whiskey and brandy. Plain water looks like gin and vodka. Beer is usually tea with a frothy soap topping. Movie "champagne" is drinkable — it's ginger ale. To keep the actors from guzzling it all between takes, one prop man used to put a dead fly in every glass.

When sound came to movies, so did sound pirates. These were people who secretly recorded sound effects from movie sound tracks. What kind of sound effects? Roaring planes, chugging trains, galloping horses, singing birds, shrieking fire engines, yelling mobs, etc. These pirated recordings were sold to sound people who worked at small radio stations.

Stars aren't born that way. Often it's a long climb to the top. Here's a list of what some of your favorites were doing before stardom struck. Would you believe . . .

Bob Hope was a boxer. He fought under the name of Packy East.

Burt Reynolds washed dishes at a restaurant in New York City.

Rock Hudson was a truck driver.

Kathleen Quinlan was a waitress.

Sly Stallone as Rocky.

Clark Gable, big ears and all.

Sylvester Stallone cleaned cages at a New York zoo.

W.C. Fields worked as a "professional drowner" at Coney Island. He'd pretend to drown, draw a crowd, and then help his boss sell hot dogs to the spectators.

George C. Scott taught at a girls' school.

Burt Lancaster was a circus acrobat.

Remember that scene in *Rocky* where Sylvester Stallone bounds to the top of those long stone steps? Remember how the camera moved right along with him with never a jiggle or bounce? Did you wonder how this was possible? After all, the cameraman had to carry his camera and run along with Stallone. The answer comes from Garrick Brown, a cameraman who specializes in impossible shots. Brown invented the SteadyCam. It's a movie camera on a mount. The mount is attached to a mechanical arm of steel and aluminum on springs. This contraption fits on a harness worn by the cameraman, leaving his hands free. There's also a small monitor fastened to the mount, so Brown can see what he's photographing while he's photographing it. The SteadyCam may sound heavy, but Brown swears it's very light. At any rate, he wasn't even puffing as he paced Rocky up those steps.

Would you believe some of the top stars flunked their first screen tests? Clark Gable bombed because the studio biggies said his ears were too big. Fred Astaire almost didn't make it because they said, "He can't act, is slightly bald, and can only dance a little."

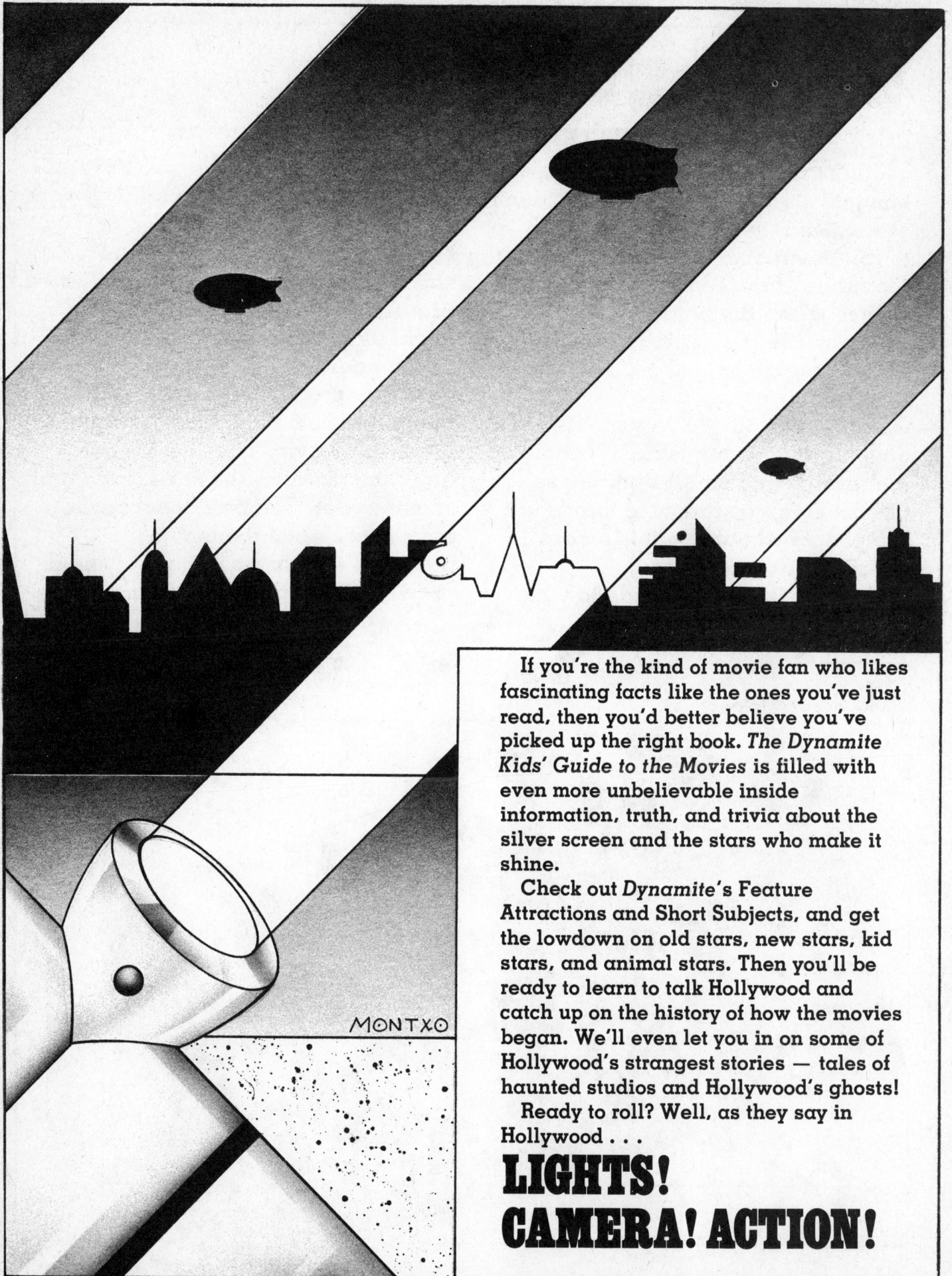

If you're the kind of movie fan who likes fascinating facts like the ones you've just read, then you'd better believe you've picked up the right book. *The Dynamite Kids' Guide to the Movies* is filled with even more unbelievable inside information, truth, and trivia about the silver screen and the stars who make it shine.

Check out *Dynamite's* Feature Attractions and Short Subjects, and get the lowdown on old stars, new stars, kid stars, and animal stars. Then you'll be ready to learn to talk Hollywood and catch up on the history of how the movies began. We'll even let you in on some of Hollywood's strangest stories — tales of haunted studios and Hollywood's ghosts!

Ready to roll? Well, as they say in Hollywood . . .

LIGHTS! CAMERA! ACTION!

Who Does What?

You're at the movies. The film has just started with a heavy action scene. And then those titles begin to roll down over the action. First the name of the film, then the stars' names. Then the producer. The director. The production designer. The names go on and on. The grip. What's a grip?

Who needs this? Every movie does. It takes a big team of people to make even a small film. Those Oscar-winning stars who thank "all the people who made this award possible" aren't kidding!

Here's a *Dynamite* guide to who does what in the movies — starting from the top — the producer.

The PRODUCER is the person behind the movie all the way. He or she comes up with the idea for the film. The idea may come from a book, play, magazine article, newspaper item — or even a song title. The producer figures out the budget — how much it will cost to make the movie. Then he or she hires the director, the stars, the screenwriter. The producer checks out every step of the movie's progress — right up to its first sneak preview. Here how it happens . . .

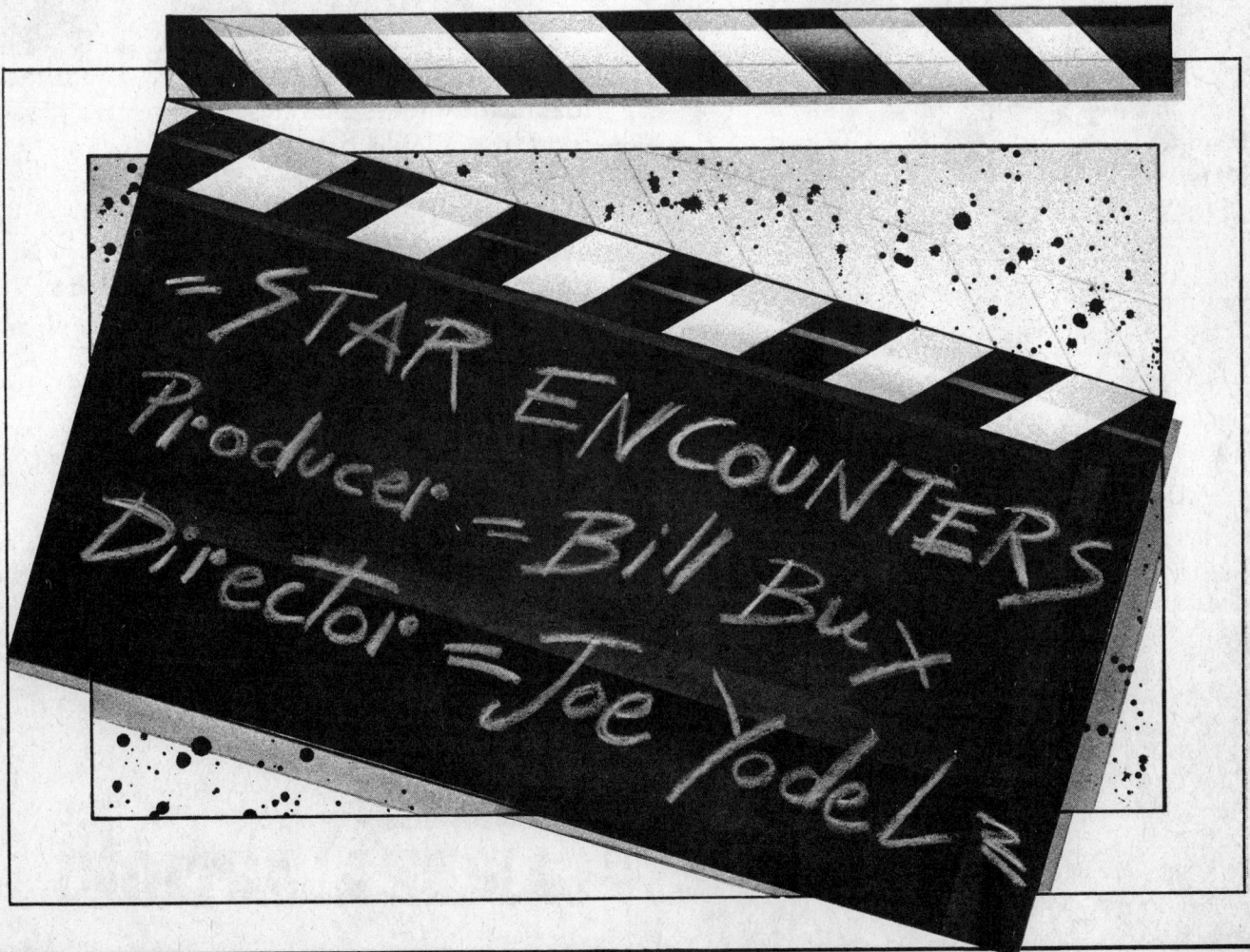

=STAR ENCOUNTERS
Producer· = Bill Bu x
Director· =Joe YodeL ≷

We fade in on a Hollywood producer named Bill Bux. (Bill is a figment of our imagination.) Since science fiction is big at the box office, Bill decides to turn *Romeo and Juliet* into a sci-fi film. He calls in **screenwriter** Louisa Typo to do a *treatment* — a summary of the movie's story.

Bill: Just follow the plot of Shakespeare's play, but set it in the future. The place is an Earth colony on Mars in the 25th century. Romeo's family has been there for a couple of generations. They've got a big mineral harvesting business going.

Louise: Shouldn't we change those names — Romeo and Juliet?

Bill: You could be right. See if you can dream up some snappier names with a futuristic twist. Remember how Luke Skywalker caught on. Oh, and you'll have to change the name of the Juliet character's parents. They're Martians. That's the conflict, see? The people from Earth hate the Martians and vice versa.

Louise: What about the ending? If you're aiming it at the teenage market, shouldn't you have an upbeat one. You know, boy gets girl and takes off for the moon?

Bill: No, let's stick with Shakespeare's ending. Boy gets girl and both die. That *Romeo and Juliet* movie was big with teenagers. Why change a winner?

Louise goes off to work on the treatment. Bill works on the movie's budget. So far he has a title for his film — *Star Encounters* — but no money to make it with. He hopes Gorgo Studios will put up the money in return for a share of the film's profits. If they aren't interested, he may be able to borrow what he needs from a bank, or from a big corporation.

As it turns out, you don't need to worry about *Star Encounters*. The people in charge of Gorgo Studios like the treatment. They just want Bill to make a few changes. They suggest that he give *Star Encounters* a happy ending and turn it into a musical. If he's willing to do this, they will raise the budget so that he can hire John Granola and Olivia Fig-Newton as stars. Bill agrees.

Next Bill chooses a **director**. Sometimes a producer and director are the same person. But Bill has never made a musical before. He picks Joe Yodel, the director of the big musical hit, *Rockpile Rock*.

Bill knows there's another advantage to hiring Yodel. The director has worked with John Granola and Olivia Fig-Newton before. Stars that big often decide which director *they* want.

As a rule, the producer and director work together on the casting to get the best actors they can afford for all the parts. One casting problem is solved if the director also happens to be the star, like Sylvester Stallone, Woody Allen, or Burt Reynolds. A star-director has a lot to say about who acts in the movie and who writes. Sometimes the star-director also writes the screenplay. Being a star-director-screenwriter means never having to say you didn't get enough lines or close-ups.

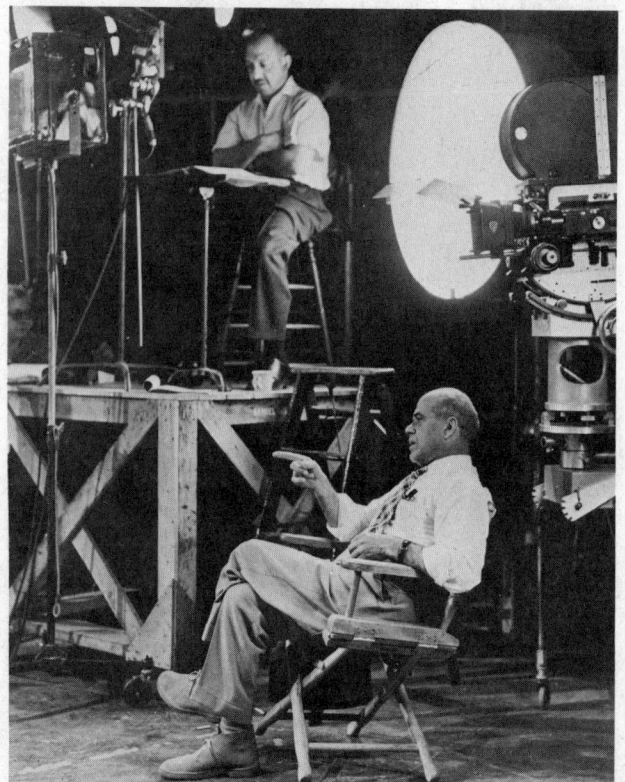

Frank Capra, a famous director, on his set.

Being a director means never having to say you haven't enough to do. The director on *Star Encounters*, as on most other films, hires the crew, choosing cameramen, sound men, electricians, carpenters, etc. He works with the screenwriter on the *shooting script* (a hammered-down version of the screenplay). He rehearses the actors in their parts, and when shooting begins, guides them through every take.

While Joe Yodel is doing all of this, our producer Bill Bux is busy in other areas. Bill picks a **set designer** who decides what kind of scenery *Star Encounters* will need. An **art director** is chosen to design the sets and see that they are built. Bill also hires a **composer** to write the music for the movie.

Meanwhile the screenwriter, Louisa, is turning the treatment of *Star Encounters* into a screenplay. This will describe the action and include the dialogue to be spoken by the actors. It may also include some camera angles.

But hard as she works, Louisa may not get all the credit for writing the screenplay when those titles roll. Another screenwriter may be hired to do special scenes. If the stars don't like what Louisa has given them to say or do, a third screenwriter could be called in to make changes.

On some movies, the job never seems to get done. The rewriting never seems to stop. Whole scenes are rewritten while the filming goes on. Actors are told to forget the lines they just learned and memorize new ones. If they can't memorize that fast, it's cue card time. John Huston, a famous director, told reporters that the screenplay was changed so often on the movie *Freud* that "We had dialogue written all over the set — on the backs of doors, on walls, on boards in front of the camera."

An elaborate indoor set with houses, sky, and a river!

Luckily this is not necessary on *Star Encounters*. In a few weeks, the script is ready and shooting starts. Some people think a movie is filmed with the scenes in order — beginning at the beginning and working right on through to the story's end. You know better. To save time and money, the scenes in which the stars appear may all be shot at first. All the outdoor scenes will be filmed when the movie goes on *location* (moves out of the studio to an outdoor setting). *Interiors*, or indoor scenes, will be shot later in sets built on the studio soundstage.

One important job that never rates publicity is **unit production manager**. No film could get very far without one. A unit production manager buys all the props (things that don't move on a movie set); gets permission from local officials to shoot outdoor scenes; pays the bills; and keeps track of how every cent is spent.

Sometime each day, *rushes* (also called "dailies") are shown to cast, crew, director, and **editor**. Rushes are the film footage taken the day before. They include every take of every scene. The director and editor decide which takes to keep, and which should be done over. You might expect the bad takes to end up in the garbage can, but very few do. Most film editors keep the discards for two reasons. The director may change his or her mind and want some of those rejects back in the film. The "bloopers" (where the actors made mistakes or blew their lines) are sometimes funny to watch.

The film editor for *Star Encounters*, Susie Scissors, gets two prints of the exposed footage. One print is of the picture, and one is of the sound. They are on separate reels that hold about 800 feet of film each.

"Some people think that once a movie is photographed, developed, and put into a can, — it's ready to show to an audience," says well-known film editor Jerry Greenberg. "But if it did work that way, no one would go to the movies. The average film would be about 100 hours long. Besides, it

A film editor at work.

wouldn't make any sense. The scenes would be all mixed up."

A film editor's job is to take thousands of feet of movie footage, and cut and splice it into a story audiences can understand. What shots will be cut out? Which ones changed around? "If an editor makes a wrong choice," says Jerry, "he can make a good movie bad. But if he knows his job, he can make a good movie look even better."

Anyone who wants to be a film editor should really like looking at movies. A thousand feet of film runs about 10 minutes. When our editor, Susie, gets the footage of *Star Encounters*, it adds up to 200,000 feet — about 35 hours long! Somehow that has to be cut down to two hours.

The editor loads every reel into a *moviola*, a mini-projection machine for one-person viewing. She cuts out shots that are fuzzy or badly lit. She rearranges the shots so that they follow the screenplay. Editors have also been known to rearrange the story. They change the order of scenes around sometimes to speed up the action, or to give the story more zip.

For weeks it's cut, splice . . . looking at the moviola's tiny screen for frames with the best angles. But even 35 hours of movie-viewing comes to an end. *Star Encounters* is now spliced into a *rough cut*. The music and titles are missing, but the action is all there.

At this point, *Star Encounters* gets its first preview. The editor, director, camera-person, and producer see it. They don't give it a rave review. They think it's too slow. They want to cut out 15 minutes more. Bill thinks two scenes should be re-shot because they are too dark. Traffic noises can be heard on the soundtrack during an outer space scene, so the sound there will have to be re-recorded.

In one shot, Olivia is shown opening an airlock with her hair hanging down her back. But when she comes through the airlock, her hair is braided on top of her head. In another, the microphone can be seen at the top of the frame. Joe wonders if maybe, just maybe, he should be directing traffic instead of movies!

So it's back to the soundstages for everybody. Scenes are re-shot to get rid of mistakes. Dialogue and sounds that have been re-recorded are put on a *wild track*, which will be cut into the right places on the movie's sound track.

Once again the editor and her assistants cut and splice. When they're finished, they have the *final cut* of *Star Encounters*.

If *Star Encounters* turns out to be a hit, guess who will get most of the credit? The director, producer, and stars. But the folks who did the following jobs rate some thanks, too. Just try getting a movie up on the screen without them. Never have so many helped to make so few look good.

A working set with lights, cameras, and actors.

Art Director — Designs the sets. Responsible for how the film "looks."

Assistant Director — Acts as the set foreman. Keeps everyone in line and generally helps the director.

Associate Producer — Helps the producer.

Bit Player — Actor with a small part.

Camera Operators — Run the cameras, load the reels.

Carpenters — Build and tear down sets.

Casting Director — Chooses actors for the director and producer to audition for parts.

Cinematographer — Directs the photography, supervises the assistant cameramen and camera operators.

Clapper Boy — Operates the clap-board before each take. The board is marked with the movie's title, the numbers of the scene and take, and the number of the camera filming the scene.

Composer — Writes movie's musical score.

Electrician — Takes care of arc lights. Arcs are big, powerful carbon lights used to light a set when filming. They are also called "brats." Don't ask us why.

Extras — People hired for crowd scenes. They don't speak lines, but when asked to make crowd noises, they say, "Rhubarb, rhubarb."

Featured Players — Actors with smaller parts and lower billing than the stars.

Gaffer — Foreman who bosses electricians. Decides where the lights should be placed on a set.

Grip — The grip department is in charge of the cameras and all the equipment needed to move the cameras. The **Key Grip** is the person in charge of this department. The second in command is called the **Best Boy.**

Makeup Artist — Can make anybody look like anything with the help of makeup, latex, and fake hair. One even made Anne Bancroft look like a gorilla!

Mixer — Controls dialogue and sound effects as they are being recorded. A super sound engineer.

Prop Master — In charge of getting any needed article — no matter how weird — for a scene. Also loads and supervises all firearms used in a movie.

Script Superviser (also known as Script Girl or Script Person) — Takes notes on all details of every scene. Keeps close track of changes in script. Keeps film "log" of everything that happens in front of cameras.

Second Unit Director — Directs the action scenes. Is often an ex-stuntman, and can act as stunt coordinator.

Stuntmen — Deserve a whole chapter to themselves. Turn to p. 32.

Technical Advisers — Doctors, lawyers, scientists, etc., hired to keep filmmakers from making laughable mistakes. For example, NASA computer experts showed the *Enterprise* crew which buttons to push in *Star Trek*. Champion bike racers trained the actors in *Breaking Away*. Not even your favorite star can know everything about everything.

Wranglers — Handle the livestock on outdoor films. Are often ex-cowboys.

Those Movie Titles

About 30 years ago, some moviemakers took a poll. They were trying to find out which words spelled winning movie titles. According to the poll, a movie title couldn't lose if it had the word *Man*, *Woman*, or *Love* in it.

Runners-up for other sure-fire title words were: *Broadway, Beauty, Black, Forbidden, Night, Dead, Danger, Wild, Fighting,* and *Secret*.

Nowadays, one-word titles are often winners. *Jaws, Alien, Hooper,* *Prophecy,* and *Moonraker* were all money-making movies. And none of those words were picked for that old-time list. Neither were words like *Star* or *Wars*.

When U.S. movies show in other countries, the titles often get changed. In Germany, *The Rescuers* was re-christened *Bernard and Bianca, the Mouse Police*. In France, it was re-titled *The Adventures of Bianca and Bernie*.

Lots of Hollywood titles get lost in the translation. Here are some more.

U.S. TITLE	FOREIGN TITLE CHANGE
Annie Hall	*Almost a Love Story* (Spain)
The Cincinnati Kid	*Table of the Devil* (Colombia)
The Heartbreak Kid	*A Change of Plans* (Latin America)
Born Free	*A Lioness of Two Worlds* (Latin America)
Butch Cassidy and The Sundance Kid	*Two Men With One Destiny* (Spain)
West Side Story	*Love Without Barriers* (Latin America)

Hong Kong fans love Hollywood movies. But do they know which Hollywood movie they're seeing? It can't be easy once the titles are translated into Chinese:

U.S. TITLE	CHINESE TITLE
Walking Tall	*You Can't Have Everything*
Tom Sawyer	*Where Bad Boys Go*
Sssssss	*The Snake Devil*
The Don Is Dead	*The Wise Gentleman Meets His Destiny*
Horror Express	*Terror on a Train*

Getting Publicity

Why would a movie company try to get in touch with a dead author?

Why would an audience wear aqualungs to watch a movie?

When wild and crazy things like these happen, you can be sure of one thing. Somebody in the movie business is trying to make you want to see a certain movie in the worst way. That somebody is called a publicist or a press agent.

The job of a movie publicist is to grab attention for a certain movie or a certain star. Most publicists go to work when the movie starts filming. They get writers from newspapers and magazines to interview the stars. They send newspaper columnists regular items about the filming. And they get the stars (and sometimes the director or producer) to go on radio and TV shows to talk about the film.

In the early days, press agents would do almost anything to make the stars look glamorous. Piper Laurie's press agent claimed she ate nothing but flowers.

Veronica Lake had to wear her hair over one eye on and off the screen.

When the movie is finished, the beat goes on. Publicists lie awake nights

MONTXO

Veronica Lake.

wondering how to turn so-so flicks into must-sees. At the premiere of *Underwater* in the 1950's, startled guests were handed aqualungs. Then they were asked to watch the movie in a king-size swimming pool.

It was as if those weird old days were back again when *Agatha* opened in 1979. The movie was about a missing 11 days in the life of mystery writer Agatha Christie. In 1925, she vanished from her home for almost two weeks. Nobody ever knew where she went, and she never told.

Agatha was filmed after Agatha Christie's death. That gave studio publicists a great idea. Why not hold a seance when the movie opened and ask Mrs. Christie where she was during those 11 days? And that's just what happened. The night that *Agatha* opened in theaters, the studio announced that a seance would

Jaws — **is the real story fishy?**

be held in California. At the stroke of midnight, a group of people would join hands. The spirit of Agatha Christie was supposed to appear and tell them the true solution to her mystery.

The spirit never showed, and the seance was a flop. But the publicists weren't ready to give up. They set up another seance for March 12 in Kansas City. Gold and black invitations went out announcing: "The spirit of Agatha is rapping for you." Two Kansas City psychics claimed they were in touch with the spirit of Mark Twain, and he would put them in touch with Agatha. He didn't.

But the seances weren't total losses.

Newspapers and radio stations mentioned the creepy goings-on. People began to wonder what *Agatha* was really all about, and went to the film to find out. And that, as they say, is show business.

Sometimes a publicity stunt backfires. At the Hollywood premiere of *Won-Ton-Ton, The Dog That Saved Hollywood*, guests could get in only if they brought a dog. The yelping of the dogs drowned out the movie, and guests went away wondering if *Won-Ton-Ton* was a dog of a film.

And now for those breaks every publicist dreams of — the ones they don't have to think up.

Remember *Towering Inferno*, the

disaster film about a fire in a skyscraper? Guess what caught fire just about the time *Towering Inferno* hit the screens? The World Trade Center, the tallest building in the U.S. Nobody was hurt, and neither was the film's business.

And now for a publicity fish story. In June, 1978, *Jaws II* opened in New York City. A few days later, Captain John Sweetman had a close encounter with a great white shark off Long Island, N.Y.

Sweetman told the newspapers that his shark was 30 feet long — just like the one in the movie. Like Quint in *Jaws*, Sweetman stuck the shark with a harpoon. It got back at him by dragging his 40-foot boat around for 14 hours.

Some people thought Universal Studios had put the captain up to his bout with the shark as a publicity stunt for *Jaws II*. Both the captain and Universal said this wasn't

so. All we know is that *Moby Dick* never got that kind of publicity break.

Not all movie publicity is meant to be read, or listened to on radios, or watched on TV. Some of it is meant to be worn. Ask yourself what movie you're advertising the next time you put on a Superman T-shirt, or a Darth Vadar mask. This kind of publicity is called merchandising — turning a movie's characters into toys, books, comic strips, and posters. Did you know a movie poster goes "gold" after it sells 500,000 copies?

Why merchandise a movie? That's not hard to figure out. Movies cost so much to make nowadays that sometimes the only way to make them pay off is to sell souvenirs. But let's look at the bright side. Someday those T-shirts and posters could be Hollywood's real golden oldies.

A blazing scene from *The Towering Inferno*.

How Movies Happened and How They Work

Did you ever wonder how movies happened? Backwards, that's how. First came the projector, then the film, and then finally the camera. It took almost 300 years for these three inventions to get together. But if you're a movie fan, you know it was worth the wait.

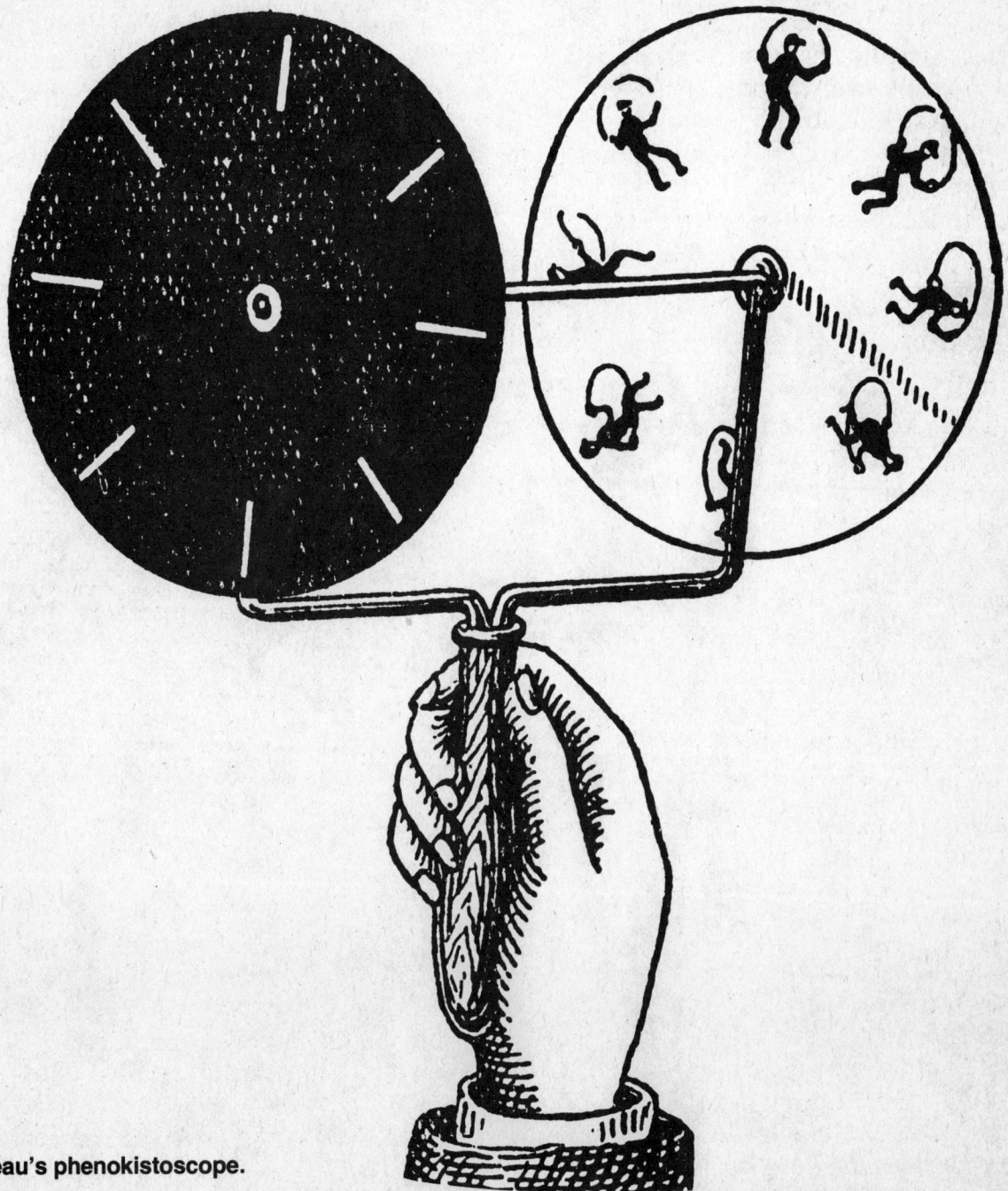

Plateau's phenokistoscope.

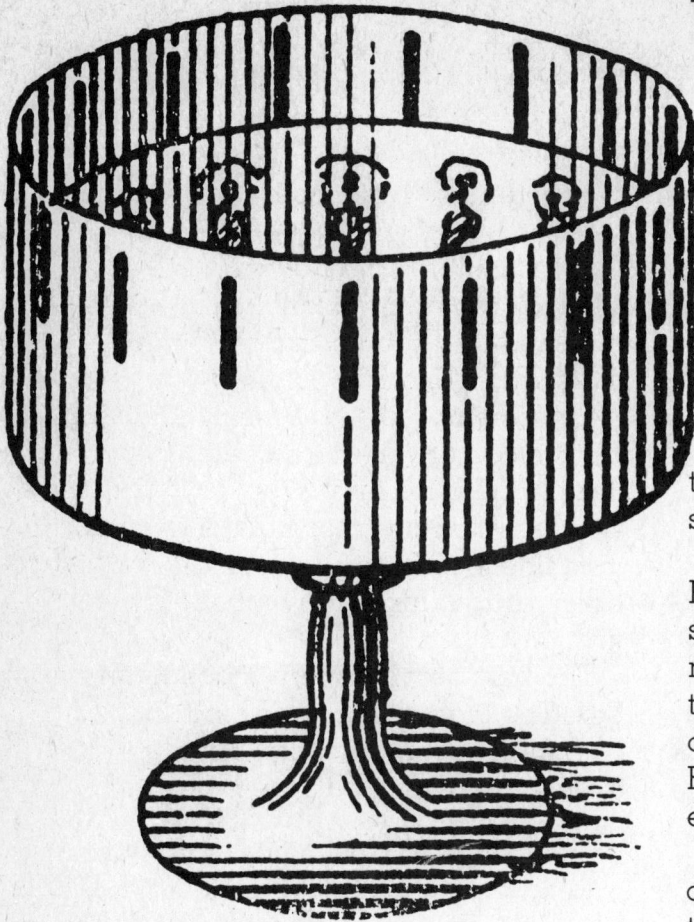

The zoetrope.

If a light bulb appears over the head of a cartoon character, you know he's about to have a bright idea. Try imagining one of those light bulbs glowing over the head of a German scientist named Athanasius Kircher in 1640. Kircher needed a way to show his students what he saw on microscope slides. So he invented a "magic lantern." It used lenses to magnify the slides and project them on a wall.

Okay, so it wasn't a *movie* projector. But it was the first step in that direction.

There was a 212-year wait for the next step. But while we're handing out light bulbs, let's give one to Joseph Plateau and his 1852 *phenokistoscope*.

The phenokistoscope had a revolving disk on each end of a metal bar. Pictures of an object in motion were painted on the inside of one disk. There were evenly spaced slots around the edge of the other disk. The idea was to spin the disks, look through the slots, and the pictures would seem to move.

In 1853, an Austrian army officer named Franz Uchatius moved the phenokisto-scope one step nearer the drive-in. He made the disk that carried the pictures transparent so light could go through it. He also fixed it so that this disk couldn't move. But a light moved behind it, lighting up each picture in turn.

Uchatius also made a change on the disk with the slots. He put lenses on it so that he could focus the pictures on a screen or wall. He called his creation "The Lantern Wheel of Life." You can call it an early movie projector.

Then there was the zoetrope, which was shaped like a bowl on a stand. The "bowl" was really a revolving cylinder. It had slots around the top and pictures around the bottom. Later, a British scientist named Clerk-Maxwell added lenses to the slots. The lenses blended the images and made them seem to move smoothly.

So far, a lot of people had figured out ways to project images and make them move — but nobody had thought of ways to *make* movies. But stick around. In the 1830's, photography was invented. After that, it was only a matter of time before movies would be born. Here are some of the events that made it happen.

1872. *Lights! Action! Camera!* Does a running horse ever have all its feet off the ground at the same time? The governor of California and some friends wanted to know. So a British photographer named Eadweard Muybridge set up a row of 24 cameras along a racetrack. Strings were tied to the lens shutter of each camera. Then the strings were stretched across the track. When the horse ran by, it broke the strings and tripped the shutters. Result: The first photographs of motion — 24 frames proving a running horse *does* have all its feet off the ground at times.

Terrific, but we're not quite ready for *Star Wars* yet. Obviously, using 24 cameras is not a practical idea. A single camera is needed that can take a succession of pictures. All through the 1880's photographers and scientists tried to tackle this problem. A French inventor named Etienne Jules Marey invented several cameras that would do the job — but they used paper film. The film was opaque (no light could go through it) so the pictures couldn't be projected. But wait!

1889. George Eastman begins to manufacture roll film. The film was made of a celluloid material that light would go through. And it could be put on sprockets so the film could be moved along and each picture brought into focus for a single moment.

1891. Double light bulbs here! The kinetograph and the kinetoscope were invented by Thomas Edison and his assistant, William Dickson.

The *kinetograph* was the first moving picture camera. It could use the new flexible celluloid film. Would you believe it was invented because Edison wanted a machine to show pictures while the phonograph (his pet invention) played music? It's true!

The kinetoscope was a machine in a box. The machine ran a 50-foot loop of 35-mm. film continuously. You peeked through an eyehole in the box to see the flickering images.

The kinetoscope, interior and exterior.

At last the film, the camera, and the projector had gotten together to produce movies. But what made movies move?

Get ready for this one. Motion pictures don't really move — your eyes fool your brain into thinking they do.

It works this way. The camera takes still photos, one at a time, on movie film. Then the film is run through the movie projector at 24 frames a second. The photos move so fast that your eyes and brain connect the separate pictures.

Scientists call this "persistence of vision." (No, that doesn't mean the kid who keeps turning around in his seat and staring at you.) Persistence of vision happens when we look at a brightly-lit object. The image of that object is "printed" on our vision for a split second. Try looking at a lighted electric bulb, then close your eyes. The image of the light bulb lingers on for a bit, even though your eyes are shut.

The same thing happens when you look at a brightly lit movie screen. A new image hits your eyes before the image you just saw fades out completely. This makes the action from one image seem to continue to the next.

That's the *how* of movies. Now back to the *what* and *when*.

In 1894, the kinetoscope went public. The first kinetoscope theater (also called a "Peepshow") opened in New York City. It looked like your average penny arcade, with banks of kinetoscope machines on either side of a center aisle. A 25-cent ticket would buy you a fast look at a few minutes of moving pictures. What can you show in a few minutes? Kinetoscope theaters showed animal acts, acrobats, Wild West stunts, jugglers, and dancers. For history buffs, there was a filmed replay of the execution of Mary, Queen of Scots. For those who wanted romance, there was *The Kiss*. It featured an overweight couple exchanging a long, long kiss.

A kinetoscope arcade in San Francisco in 1899.

Would you pay a quarter to watch *Fred Ott's Sneeze?* Would you believe it was one of the early hits of the kinetoscope theaters? This minute-and-a-half movie was the first film made by William Dickson, the fellow who helped Edison work out the kinetograph and the kinetoscope. The star of *Sneeze* was a mechanic who worked for Edison. His big talent was being able to sneeze on command.

There were movie censors in those days, too. One kinetoscope featured a Spanish dancer named Carmencita. The swirling flounces of her skirt showed a glimpse of her ankles. Those ankles got the film banned in Newark, N.J., because the censor feared seeing them "might bring a blush to the cheeks" of viewers.

Most of these early kinetoscope movies were made in Edison's "studio" in West Orange, N.J. The studio was about the size of a boxing ring. It was called the "black Maria" because it looked like the wagons used to take prisoners to jail. It was actually a tarpaper-covered shed on wheels. The "Black Maria" was the world's first movie studio. But it soon had plenty of competition.

1895. Meanwhile, foreign movies were getting into the act. The Lumière Brothers of Lyon, France, took movies one step further. On December 28, 1895, they

The Lumière Brothers.

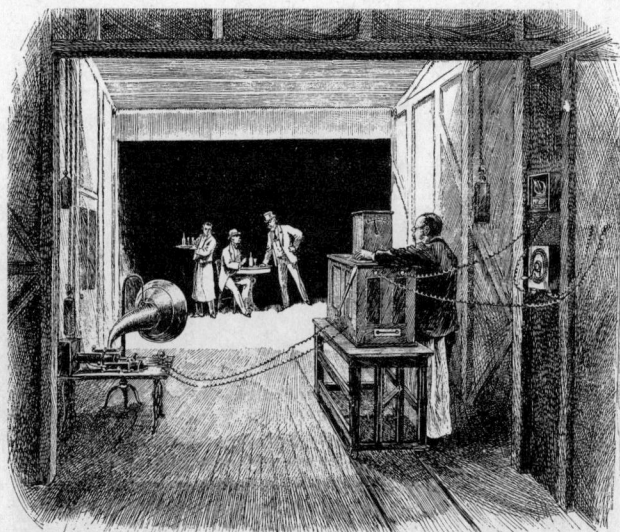
Edison's "movie studio."

projected a film onto a screen so that a whole audience could watch the action at the same time.

Their invention, the cinematograph, made movies easier to watch. Until then, projected images were often jumpy, blurry, or out of focus. In fact, some of them were so hard on the eyes that they were used as "chasers" at the end of vaudeville shows to chase audiences out of the theaters so new customers could come in.

The Lumières also invented a portable hand-cranked camera you could use anywhere. Until then, movie cameras were fastened down in one spot. They could pan (move from left to right or vice versa). But panning was the only real camera movement. Chalk marks on the floor showed the actors where to stand. If they moved off the marks, they moved out of the picture.

1896. The Lumières' success made Edison realize that a machine that went one-on-one with a viewer was not the way to build big audiences. What he needed was a projector that could show big pictures on a screen in a theater full of people.

Luckily, there was such a projector. Edison didn't even have to invent it. It had been invented by Thomas Armat. Edison began manufacturing these projectors, which were called vitascopes.

In 1896, Edison gave New Yorkers a new thrill. Using the vitascope, he projected movies on a big screen at Bial's Music Hall. The audience saw waves crashing on a beach, a few rounds from a prize fight, and a scene from a play.

The vitascope made our present-day movie theaters possible. The first theaters were called nickelodeons because it only cost five cents to get into them. The price was right, because nickelodeons were short on comfort. All it took to start a nickelodeon was an empty store, a projector, a screen, and some folding chairs.

The early movies were a little low on plot. One early biggie showed a train leaving a station. Another flick showed workers leaving a factory. Nobody made a movie of audiences leaving a theater, but that's what was happening. People were bored just watching objects move. They wanted movies that told (or showed) a story. In 1902 they got one called *A Trip to the Moon*, made by a French magician named Georges Méliès. It had a show-stopper of a scene in which explorers got into a rocketship and were shot by cannon right into the eye of the Man in the Moon.

Strangely enough, Méliès tried to buy the rights to the cinematograph from the

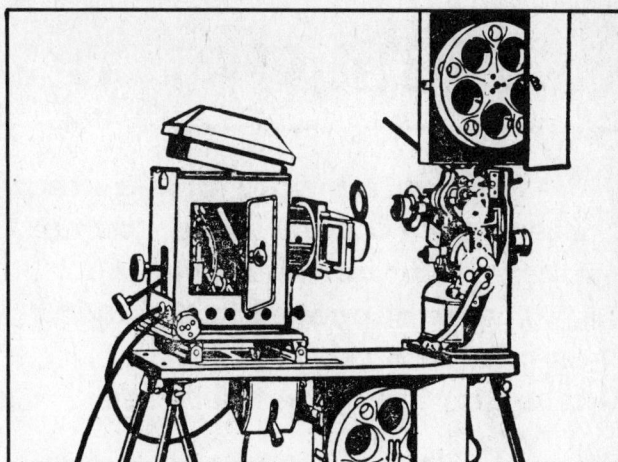
Edison's projecting kinetoscope.

Lumières. They said no. Antoine Lumière thought movies were only a passing fad and that Méliès would be wasting his money!

Méliès was the father of special effects. One day he was shooting a street scene in Paris. His camera jammed and it was a couple of minutes before he got it started again. When he projected the day's work, he saw a bus appear to turn into a hearse. Today this is known as stop-motion photography. The camera stopped as the bus went by, then started up as a hearse appeared.

With stop motion, Méliès discovered he could make objects seem to disappear and reappear — as if by magic. He also learned how to do slow motion, double exposures, dissolves, and fades. He liked to get into the act, too. In one of his films, he played the role of a magician whose head explodes.

Once movies began to look better and tell stories, audiences flocked back to theaters. Business was booming, but moviemakers knew it was only a matter of time before new gimmicks would be needed to keep the paying customers in their seats. One of those gimmicks was sound. The first talking picture wasn't seen and heard by moviegoers until 1927. But what most movie audiences didn't know was that "talkies" had been around since 1889.

A scene from Méliès's *Trip to the Moon.*

Sounding Off

Movie theaters were once a great place to take a nap. There was no spoken dialogue. Whatever the actors were supposed to be saying was printed on title cards that flashed on the screen between action shots. Title cards also told the audience when and where the film was supposed to be taking place. The only noise came from the audience, especially when they read the titles out loud to each other.

Most people think the first talking movie was *The Jazz Singer*. But sound was around as early as October 6, 1889. On that day, strange things were happening in Thomas Edison's laboratory. Edison's assistant, William Dickson, had planned a little surprise. He ran tubes from Edison's phonograph, and put them in Edison's ears. Then he started up a movie of himself on a little four-foot screen.

Through the tubes, Edison heard Dickson say, "Good morning, Mr. Edison, glad to see you back. I hope you like the kinetophone. I will lift my hand and count up to ten." And he did. The sound from the phonograph more or less matched Dickson's lip movements.

Edison thought the kinetophone was where the movie action was going to be. For 24 years, he kept trying to synchronize records on the phonograph with pictures on the screen. But when he showed the kinetophone in public in 1913, the audience laughed and booed.

No doubt about it — the kinetophone had "bugs" that Edison hadn't managed to iron out. If the actors didn't stand right up next to the microphone, their voices sounded like Donald Duck's. But what kind of a drama could you have with the actors rooted to one spot? So Edison tried recording the dialogue on a separate record. The record would be played on a phonograph placed behind the movie screen.

Guess who had to synchronize the action on the screen with the phonograph? The projectionist, that's who. He was supposed to do this by stopping and starting the phonograph with ropes and pulleys. Everything went wrong. The sound kept going off because the ropes kept breaking. The audience kept complaining that the volume was too low to hear what the actors were saying.

Edison worked two more years, trying to make the kinetophone a non-laughing-stock. Finally he gave the whole thing up.

Meanwhile, another scientist named Lee De Forest had found a better way. He invented a vacuum tube in 1906. With this tube, sound could be amplified so that it was loud enough to be heard throughout a movie theater. Then in 1923 he invented a method of recording sound right onto movie film.

Unfortunately, movies that talked were something Hollywood didn't want to hear about. They already had hundreds of silent films in production. They had even more hundreds showing around the world. What's more, all those movie theaters weren't equipped to show talkies. Putting in sound would cost money nobody wanted to spend.

But just try and hold back progress! While De Forest and others were working on recording sound on film, Bell Telephone Company was still working on a combination record and film. Finally in 1925, they got the synchronization down and they were able to sell their invention, the vitaphone, to Warner Brothers Studio. Why? Because Warner's films weren't doing well at the box office. They needed a gimmick to bring in the customers — and that gimmick was sound.

On October 6, 1927, Warner Brothers showed *The Jazz Singer*, the first full-length movie in which an actor talked. It was exactly 38 years to the day since William Dickson ran his "talkie" for Thomas Edison.

The Jazz Singer was only partly a talkie. The audience heard four songs and a few lines of dialogue. But Al Jolson, the star, made motion-picture history when he told the audience, "You ain't heard nothin' yet, folks!" He was so right.

Warner's Theatre in New York City.

Some Fabulous Movie Firsts

The first American movie to tell a story was *The Great Train Robbery*, produced in 1903 by Edwin S. Porter. It was also the first Western, the first box-office hit, and it featured the first movie star — Bronco Billy. (Billy's real name was Max Aronson.)

Hollywood first went West in 1907. That was the year filmmakers decided to trade in New York and New Jersey for California's balmy climate. But Hollywood itself dates back to 1883. In that year a Kansas couple named Wilcox bought some California farmland for $1.25 an acre. Mrs. Wilcox named the place after two holly trees in her front yard. Yes, fans, she called it Hollywood — *the* Hollywood.

The first American movie serial was the 1914 *Perils of Pauline*. It starred Pearl White. Every episode ended with Pearl in deadly danger. Sometimes she was even shown hanging by her fingernails from a cliff — and that's why serials came to be called "cliffhangers." You had to go back to the theater the following week to see the next chapter, showing how Pauline got out of her last pickle. Serials were usually divided into 15 or 20 chapters, lasting about 20 minutes each.

The first Hollywood studio was the Nestor Film Company, built in 1911. Location: an ex-tavern at Sunset Boulevard and Gower Street.

A typical scene from *The Perils of Pauline.*

The first animal star was a dog named Strongheart.

The first monster movie was *The Lost World*, a 1925 epic starring rubber dinosaurs. These prehistoric terrors were miniatures created by special-effects genius Willis O'Brien. (Willis also created the 1933 *King Kong*.) They had wire veins, movable wooden skeletons, and hidden air bladders that made them seem to breathe.

The first film used to make most movies was cellulose nitrate film. The older nitrate film gets, the easier it catches fire or fades. So the Library of Congress is working around the clock to copy those old movies onto modern safety film. But there are some old movies they want to copy and can't because they can't get the originals. The Most Wanted List includes: *Greed*; the 1917 version of *Cleopatra*; the 1922 *Beyond the Rocks*, starring Rudolph Valentino; the 1923 *Battle of the Century*, starring Laurel and Hardy; and Thomas Edison's 1912 version of *Frankenstein*.

The first Hollywood premiere for a movie trailer was held on June 27, 1979. Guests got just enough popcorn to get them through two minutes of coming attractions from *The Jerk*, starring Steve Martin. The show was bigger outside the theater. Stars pulled up in limousines and did celebrity interviews on the sidewalk. Cheering fans wore rabbit ears and arrows-through-the-forehead in honor of Steve.

Dinosaur from *The Lost World*.

How To Talk Hollywood

How would you like to be framed, shot, cut, and spliced? It could happen. In fact, it happens all the time to your favorite stars.

Moviemakers have a language all their own — and you're about to get your first lesson in it.

Angle — Position of the camera when it's filming. Camera angles can include high and low angles, close-ups and long shots, etc.

Boom — Crane attached to a camera platform so the camera can be lifted high above the action.

Cast — Performers in a movie.

Close-up — Camera angle where the subject fills the frame. Those wall-to-wall shots of actors' faces are close-ups.

Crab dolly — Has nothing to do with cute seafood. This is a platform on wheels that can be pushed around. A movie camera is mounted on it.

Cut — It can mean "Stop filming!" It's also what a *cutter*, or editor, does when choosing and arranging shots into a finished movie.

Dissolve — When one scene in a movie seems to melt into the next one.

Dolly shot — The shot taken by a camera when it moves up toward or moves away from the actors.

Double exposure — A shot in which one image is seen over another. It happens when two parts of a scene are shot separately, then projected together.

Dubbing — Mixing the sound tracks of a movie. Adding music and sound effects to the dialogue track so that every sound comes in the right place in the finished movie.

Edit — To look at all the film that's been shot, select the frames to use, then cut up and splice together a movie.

Fade-in — When a screen image slowly appears out of total darkness. A *fade-out* works the other way. The shot slowly disappears into darkness.

Footage — Number of feet of exposed film. (In other words, film that's been shot.)

Frame — Single picture on a strip of film.

Location — Any place outside a studio where part or all of a movie is filmed.

Long shot — The opposite of a close-up. A long shot shows the entire scene.

Medium shot — A camera shot that shows more than a close-up and less than a long shot.

Pan — A shot in which the camera moves across a scene, filming it from one side to the other.

Prescore — To record the music for a movie before the movie starts shooting.

Reflector — Shiny surface (a polished flat piece of metal, for example) used to bounce light onto props or actors.

Running shot — Shot taken as the camera moves neck-and-neck alongside a moving object or actor.

Score — Music composed for a movie. When music is *scored*, it is recorded on a sound track.

Set — Place in which a movie scene is filmed.

Shoot — To film a scene.

Shot — Smallest part of a movie scene. It takes more than one shot to make a *scene*, and several scenes to make a *sequence*.

Splice — To join two ends of two frames together.

Sleeper — Low budget movie that turns out to be a hit.

Synchronizer — Machine used by the film editor to match the picture and the sound track.

Take — A scene of a movie being photographed at a given time. It usually takes several "takes" or tries before a director is satisfied with the scene.

Wipe — Camera trick in which scene seems to be erased from the screen.

Zoom — When a wide-angle shot changes suddenly to a close-up.

The Wild World of Stunting

They fall out of planes, windows, and off horses and mountains. They leap from tall building to building in a single bound. They crash in cars and run around in flames. But if you ask movie stuntmen or stuntwomen what they do for a living, they will say, "Gags."

Maybe you thought a gag was a joke. To a stunt person, a gag is a carefully planned stunt.

Nothing gets a stunt person riled up faster than hearing somebody say, "Movie stunts? Oh, they're all fakes." If it's a stunt, it's no fake. Stunts are for-real dangerous acts, performed by actors with special know-how.

For many years, Hal Needham was Hollywood's most famous and highest paid stuntman. "There are some stunts," says Hal, "where if you make a wrong choice, they'll be walking slow and singing low behind you. There are some you do without a lot of thinking — like sliding cars around, or laying a motorcycle down. But for the tough ones, you put in an awful lot of planning."

Needham rates two of his stunts as extra tough. One was jumping a truck across a lake. For extra push, the truck had a rocket fastened under it. "I had to figure out how long the ramp was, what the truck weighed, and what force the rocket had." All that math could take the fun out of any gag.

A spectacular car stunt from *Hooper*.

Needham's other choice in the tough stunt sweepstakes was jumping from the back of one running horse to the back of another hitched to a stagecoach. "Alan Gibbs and I did that gag in *Little Big Man*. We spent six months training ourselves and the horses. Then we did it 12 times in front of the camera so all the angles would be on film."

Needham directed *Hooper*, a movie about stunt people. "Almost every daredevil stunt ever shown in films is in *Hooper*," he says proudly. The movie starred Burt Reynolds, an ex-stuntman. To show he hadn't forgotten how to work out a gag, Reynolds did some of the stunts in *Hooper* himself. For example, he jumped out of a helicopter onto an airbag. But the hairiest *Hooper* stunt — jumping a car across a bridge that's been washed out — was done by full-time stuntmen A.J. Bakunas and Buddy Joe Hooker.

Bakunas got $1,000 for each of the four stunts he did in *Hooper*. "I love the job," he once said. "When other stuntmen don't want to do a gag because it's too risky, they call me. I never turn down a job. But if I told you I wasn't jittery before a stunt, I'd be lying. It's good for a stuntman to be a little scared. It makes him careful and not too overconfident. Some people say I'm crazy to keep doing stunts. I don't think it's any crazier than working eight hours a day in a stuffy office."

Unfortunately, Bakunas's story has a sad ending. In 1979, he was doing a 323-foot free-fall for a movie called *Steel*. The airbag he planned to land on burst, and Bakunas was killed.

In the old days of silent movies, most actors were expected to do their own stunts. The price for risking life and limb was seldom right. When Cecil B. DeMille directed *Intolerance*, he hired 2,000 extras to be run down by chariots and crushed under falling walls. For this, each extra was paid $1.25 a day, plus lunch and carfare.

The Keystone Kops did a little better.

They made $3.00 a day for doing their own stunts. In 1914, they won a "hazardous duty" pay raise — $5.00 a day.

When King Kong climbed a skyscraper, it was a camera trick. When Harold Lloyd climbed one, it was for real. Lloyd was famous for playing timid nice guys who always got into dangerous stunts. He made hundreds of two-reel comedies. One stunt that was a Harold Lloyd "special" was climbing up the side of a building. Lloyd would never use a double, and did the climbing himself. He had a safety net placed far below, out of sight of the camera. He never fell, but if he had, he would probably have been hurt or killed. One day, just for laughs, he dropped a dummy out of a skyscraper window. The dummy bounced off the platform and crash-dived to the street below.

Serials about damsels in distress were big in the silent days, and the serial damsels did all their own stunts. And what stunts they were! Here's what Helen Gibson had to do in *The Hazards of Helen*.

Harold Lloyd out on a limb.

1) Chase after a runaway freight train on a motorcycle; 2) crash the motorcycle through a wooden gate; and 3) zoom the cycle up a station platform, through the open doors of a boxcar, and land on the flatcar of a passing train.

Luckily Helen was a trained acrobat before she became a serial star. So was Pearl White, star of *The Perils of Pauline*. Pearl was a whiz at jumping off bridges and onto trains below. But one stunt Pearl pulled really had audiences gasping. The scene showed her menaced by rats while trapped in a mill being flooded with rising water. What audiences didn't know was that the water was all Pearl had to worry about. The rats were old and toothless.

Nowadays studios don't like big stars to risk their necks doing stunts. Remember the scene where Paul Newman and Robert Redford jumped from a cliff into a river in *Butch Cassidy and The Sundance Kid*? Here's what you really saw. Redford and Newman jumped a few feet off a low "cliff" to a platform below for a close-up. Two stuntmen did the 70-foot dive from a crane for the long shot.

Stuntman Remy Julienne specializes in car jumps and car crashes. Nobody can make a car somersault the way Julienne can. He does this by varooming off a 15-foot ramp. The car flips over because there's a cable hooked to its front end. If Julienne is lucky, the car will then land on a ten-foot stack of cardboard cartons. So far he's been lucky.

"Car stunts have gotten more dangerous," says stunt coordinator Ron Rondell.

The famous leap from Butch Cassidy and the Sundance Kid.

"It used to be that nobody would have even tried to roll a car over more than a couple of times. Now with cannons, cars can be turned over nine or ten times on flat ground."

A cannon is a big cylinder with a powder charge inside. It is welded under the car with the muzzle pointing at the road. The stuntman zooms the car down the stretch, then throws it sideways. At the same time he pushes a button to fire the cannon. The cannon goes off, pushing a metal pole into the ground. The pole flips the car over . . . and over . . . and over . . .

Who thinks up the stunts you see on screen? The guilty party is usually the stunt coordinator. Stunt coordinators design the gags to fit the action in the screenplay. They check out the camera angles, lenses, camera speeds. They also hire the stunt people — but they may decide to do the toughest stunts themselves. And they know how, because stunt coordinators are ex-stunt people.

Stunt coordinators earn about $200,000 a year. Stunt people are paid on an average of $60,000. But money isn't everything. A lot of stunt people don't think they get the credit they deserve for making movies so exciting.

"The stars think a stuntman is just a little above an extra," says stuntman Dick Grace. "The producers think he's a little below a moron. The public has never heard of him. They think all the thrills are faked."

Why pick such a dangerous way to make a living? "Why not?" says Hal Needham. "It's fun if you live through it. Besides, a lot of us figure that if we stick with it, we might someday get a chance to play a human being."

Hal has never felt underpaid. For dropping out of an airplane and landing on top of a galloping horseman, he got $1,500. If he had missed, that would barely have covered his hospital bills. But Hal says he has never been hurt doing a fall. His secret? "I stay loose," he says, "looser than warm spaghetti."

And then there's Frank McGrath, a real daredevil. Frank has jumped out of burning buildings and moving trains. He's crashed cars and planes. He once jumped a horse across a 125-foot chasm. But the only time he got hurt was the day he broke a leg getting out of a parked car.

Great Words from the Movies

Charles Boyer romances Hedy Lamarr in *Algiers*.

Some lines from movies will live forever. Who could forget the way Scarlet O'Hara said "fiddle de dee" or the way R2D2 said "beep beep" — or these great words:

ROMANCE

Come with me to the Casbah. (*Algiers*, 1938)

Don't ask for the moon! We have the stars! (*Now Voyager*, 1942)

MYSTERY

Do you believe the dead come back to watch the living? (*Rebecca*, 1940)

There are some things man was not meant to know. (*The Invisible Ray*, 1936.)

If you knew him, you'd know he couldn't possibly be a murderer! [and . . .]

If you want to stay here, you'd better not be too curious. (Both quotes from *The Invisible Ghost*, 1941)

Feet, do your stuff! (*Revenge of the Zombies*, 1943)

SCIENCE FICTION

All the universe or nothing! Which shall it be? (*Things To Come*, 1936)

An intellectual carrot? The mind boggles! (*The Thing*, 1951)

Synthetic Flesh! Synthetic Flesh! (*Doctor X*, 1932)

WORLD WAR II

Oh, Victor, please don't go to the underground meeting tonight! (*Casablanca*, 1943)

Humphrey Bogart and Ingrid Bergman in *Casablanca*.

COMEDY

Either this guy died, or my watch has stopped. (*A Day at the Races*, 1937)

You've got the brain of a four-year-old boy, and I'll bet he was glad to get rid of it. (*Horse Feathers*, 1932)

Here's another fine mess you've gotten me into. (Any Laurel and Hardy comedy)

SPORTS

Let's win one for the Gipper! (*Knute Rockne*, 1940)

There can only be one winner, folks. But isn't that the American way? (*They Shoot Horses, Don't They?* 1969)

WEIRD STUFF

Wrong? What could be wrong with our child, Robert? (*The Omen*, 1976)

Easy enough to talk of soul and spirit and essential worth, but not when you're three feet high. (*The Incredible Shrinking Man*, 1957)

Now here are a group of sayings that turn up over and over again in movies. These are the classic lines — ones you've heard before, and you'll probably hear again in movies that haven't even been made yet.

WESTERNS

So you're the great (Jesse James, Billy the Kid, Bat Masterson, Wyatt Earp). Let's see if you're as fast a draw as they say.

We'll head 'em off at the pass.

What's a nice girl like you doing in a place like this?

The Marx Brothers in *A Day at the Races*.

Boris Karloff *is* **the curse of the Pharaoh's tomb.**

MYSTERY

I've called you all here to tell you that I've changed my will.

Those old curses are only superstition. I don't care — I'm going to enter the Pharaoh's tomb.

The men say this place is taboo. They say we must go back.

ADVENTURE

Haven't you ever wondered what's on the other side of that mountain?

You're going out there a raw recruit — and you're coming back a hero!

What seems to be the trouble, Captain?

MUSICALS

You're going out there a green kid, and you're coming back a star!

WORLD WAR II

We have ways to make you talk.

The chorus line in *Forty-Second Street*.

Kid Stuff

Being a kid has its ups and downs — but being a kid movie star must be good times forever. Is that the way it looks to you? Money piling up in the bank? Fans asking for autographs? Your name up there in lights? Your face up there on the big screen?

Sounds great, doesn't it? And for some young stars it has been. But for others, stardom was anything but good times. Take what happened to Jackie Coogan.

Jackie was born in 1914. His parents were in vaudeville, and Jackie was trouping with them by the time he was three. One night he was onstage dancing his little heart out when Charlie Chaplin happened to be in the audience. What happened next was like a movie. Charlie was looking for a cute little tyke to play opposite him in *The Kid*. And Jackie was the cutest little tyke he ever saw.

So Jackie, aged six, got a contract and a trip to Hollywood. *The Kid* turned out to be a big hit, and Jackie became a big star. Fans called him "the greatest boy actor in the world." His star's salary made him the highest paid.

Now comes the bad part. Jackie's mother and father "took care" of the thousands of dollars he earned. Over the years it added up to about four million. But when Jackie grew up and tried to collect some of his earnings, his parents threw him out of the house. He had to sue to collect even part of all those millions.

A lot of people were pretty shocked over what happened to Jackie. So was the California State Legislature. It got busy and passed the Child Actor's Bill — also known as the Coogan Bill. This law makes sure that at least half of what any child actor earns is put away in a trust fund. When the star grows up, only he or she can spend that money.

Jackie wasn't the only child actor to get ripped off in the old days. Darla Hood, one of the gang in the *Our Gang* comedies, pulled down $750 a week for six years. She never got to spend a cent of it. It all went to support her family because the only Hood working was little Darla.

The richest child movie star in history is Tatum O'Neal. That's because she not only got $350,000 for her work in the hit film *The*

Jackie Coogan and Charlie Chaplin in *The Kid*.

Darla Hood in Our Gang.

Bad News Bears, but she also got nine percent of the film's profits.

Tatum always had a way with money. In her first movie, *Paper Moon*, she had to be bribed to learn her lines. Short lines she learned for 50 cents. Long speeches cost director Peter Bogdanovich 50 dollars each.

But money can't buy everything. Even if you're a rich kid star, it can't buy you out of getting an education. If you're of school age, you've still got to go to school even when you're making a movie. The law says so.

How do you go to school if you're acting all day? The movie company hires a tutor to be with you on the set. At least four hours per day must be spent on school work. The tutor teaches you between takes and after the day's shooting is finished. You have to take tests and get good grades. What's more, when the adult actors get to go home and rest, you get to do your homework *and* learn your lines for the next day's work.

One of the problems that child actors have to face is growing up. As time marches on, it has a way of making a kid too old to play kids and too young to play adult roles. A lucky few manage to hang on to their careers as they get older.

Robert Blake is a good example of this kind of staying power. He was born Mickey Gubitosi in 1933 in Nutley, New Jersey. His parents got him parts in stage plays when he was only two. At the age of eight he was playing an Indian named Little Beaver in the *Red Ryder* movie series. Little Beaver was a sort of pint-size Tonto.

At 15, Mickey changed his name and his style. As Robert Blake, he played a Mexican boy in *The Treasure of the Sierra Madre*. About that time his luck also changed — for the worse. He had trouble with drugs. He was expelled from school.

But all's well that ends well. Once Bob grew up, he became a real star. He played leads in *Tell Them Willie Boy Is Here*, *In Cold Blood*, and *Electra Glide in Blue*. Then came the title role in the TV series

Tatum O'Neal in The Bad News Bears.

Baretta. Nobody had to tell the television audience that Robert Blake was here!

Have you ever wondered what became of Lee Lio Loong? Have you ever heard of Lee Lio Loong? Between the ages of six and 18, he was the top kid star in Hong Kong movies. Then Lee Lio Loong vanished forever — only to reappear in California as Bruce Lee. You probably know the rest of that story.

Nancy Drew fans, does the name Bonita Granville ring any bells? It should, because Bonita starred in four Nancy Drew movies between 1938 and 1939. The films were: *Nancy Drew, Detective; Nancy Drew, Reporter; Nancy Drew, Trouble Shooter;* and *Nancy Drew and the Hidden Staircase.*

Bonita was only 15 and 16 when she played Nancy, and it was a real change of pace for her. From the age of 13 she had always played heavies. She got an Academy Award nomination for playing a really rotten kid in *These Three*. That led to

Bonita Granville as Nancy Drew.

her playing a 17th-century juvenile delinquent in *Maid of Salem* (1936), and the title role in *Beloved Brat* (1938). "I really like playing the villain," said Bonita, just before she switched to Nancy Drew.

Where is Bonita now? Alive and well and living in Texas. As Bonita Wrather, she co-produced the latest *Lassie* movie in 1978.

Lassie also had a paw in the career of Elizabeth Taylor. Liz was just 11 when she starred in her first flick, *Lassie Come Home*, in 1943. If it's hard for you to imagine Liz as a child star, that's because you haven't been watching enough old movies on TV. She's the pretty little girl in the 1944 version of *Jane Eyre* and the 1944 *National Velvet*.

A lot of young stars have turned out to be old pros when it comes to Academy Awards. Jackie Cooper was the first kid to get an Academy Award nomination in 1931 for his work in *Skippy*. He was nine. Hayley Mills won a special Oscar in 1960.

Bruce Lee as a grown-up star.

She was 15. Why didn't they give her a "Best Actress" award? Nobody knows. But it was as though Hollywood said to Hayley: "You always turn in a top performance, even when the movies you're in aren't very good."

Patty Duke, however, did get an Oscar for "Best Supporting Actress" in 1962 for her role as Helen Keller in *The Miracle Worker*. She had to share the award with her co-star, Anne Bancroft.

The youngest Oscar winner of all has to be Tatum O'Neal. At the ripe old age of 10, she hit the top by walking off with a 1973 Academy Award for playing a cigarette-smoking, wise-cracking con kid in *Paper Moon*. Her Oscar went up on the mantelpiece of her home. For show? "No," said Tatum firmly. "For hanging my frisbee on."

Elizabeth Taylor and Mickey Rooney in *National Velvet*.

Back in the nickelodeon days, these messages often appeared between features:

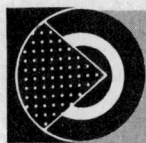

Ladies,
Please Remove Your Hats.

Please Read the Titles
to Yourself.
Reading Them Aloud
Annoys Others.

One Moment Please. Operator Is Changing the Film.

Please Don't Do Anything Here You Wouldn't Do in Your Living Room.

That Includes Spitting on the Floor.

The Secret Lives of Hollywood's Animal Stars

A star is born. He fizzles out after his first big hit. It's an old Holly- **wood story, but it shouldn't happen to a dog. The trouble is, it did.**

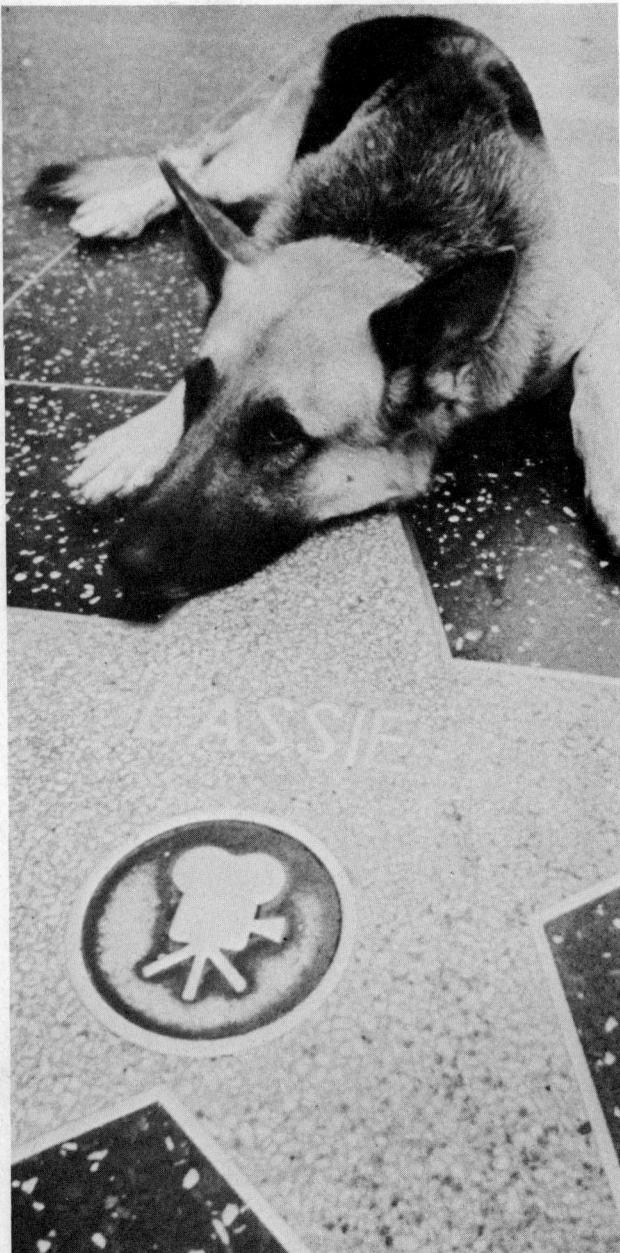

Won Ton Ton.

The dog was a German shepherd named Augustus (Gus) Von Schumacher. He belonged to animal trainer Karl Miller. He earned his dog biscuits as a stand-in for the dog star of a TV show called *Run, Joe, Run.*

Gus never expected stardom to strike him, but it did. Paramount Studios needed a dog who looked like silent-screen dog hero Rin-Tin-Tin. Gus was a dead ringer. He took a screen test and won the title role in *Won-Ton-Ton, The Dog That Saved Hollywood.*

At first there was the build-up. They started calling Gus "the Robert Redford of dog actors." He was invited on TV talk shows. He escorted starlets to premieres.

But Gus wasn't enjoying himself much. He had to diet to keep his weight down to 96 pounds. The rest of the cast complained that he gave them fleas. The action called for him to do stunts such as balancing on the wings of a biplane. In another scene he had to jump on the back of a galloping horse. "If you worked a human actor that hard, he'd quit," said co-star Bruce Dern.

Gus may have wanted to quit, but he was a trouper. "He's a pro," said director Michael Winner. "He always turns up for work on time. He doesn't nag me with questions about why he's doing anything, or what he's supposed to be thinking about while he does it. The only trouble with Gus is that he won't go out to lunch with you. And at the end of the day, you can't call him up for a chat."

After all that hard work, the movie bombed. And so did Gus's career. He retired. But the experience wasn't a total loss. In *Won-Ton-Ton*, he had learned how to crash through a door. Whenever Miller tried to keep him from sleeping in the master bedroom, Gus crashed.

Some dogs are big enough to sleep anywhere they want to. In the case of Rin-Tin-Tin, that meant sleeping in his own king-size bed. Not even Lee Duncan, his owner, was going to argue with the most popular dog star in movie history.

According to Hollywood legend, Rinty was discovered on a World War I battlefield, where he had been abandoned by German troops. Was this true? Maybe not. Lee Duncan also told a friend that Rinty found *him* on a Hollywood street and followed him home.

Unlike most dogs, Rinty could arrange his face to show big-screen emotions. "Grief, hope, courage, patience — he could express all these emotions better than a lot of human actors," said Duncan.

It was true. In his big movie, *The Night Cry*, audiences burst into tears when Rinty looked up at the camera after being unjustly accused of killing a sheep. Rin-Tin-Tin made a lot of movie serials with Rex, the King of the Wild Horses. Off camera, Rex was a real meanie who liked to kick his co-stars around. Rex was also afraid of heights. If the role called for him to gallop to the edge of a cliff or slide down a mountainside, Rex called in sick.

While Rin-Tin-Tin worked, he pulled down $1,500 a week, plus five percent of the gross. He retired rich and lived to a ripe old age. But his fans may not have known this because his son, Rin-Tin-Tin, Jr., took his place on the screen. Junior was followed by Rin-Tin-Tin III and IV, who appeared in TV serials and commercials in the 1970's. But not one of his descendants had Rinty's star quality.

They call Rin-Tin-Tin the Clint Eastwood of dog stars, because he was strong and silent. But the star of all those Lassie movies broke into films because he was noisy and liked to chase cars.

He? Yes, fans, Lassie was really a he. His first owner couldn't stand all that yapping and chasing, so he sold the collie to movie animal trainer Rudd Weatherwax for $70.

Weatherwax knew MGM was looking for a collie to play the title role in *Lassie Come Home*. "They wanted a female," recalls Weatherwax, "but the only one that tested out was shedding so much that she looked small and gaunt. My dog had a rich, full coat. For the test, they had him do a scene where he swam 100 yards, rolled over, and collapsed. He was a smash, so they decided he could play a her."

Lassie's only bad habit was that he loved chasing cars. But Weatherwax didn't care. "If we had a scene where Lassie was supposed to make an escape, we'd put a car on the set just out of camera range. Lassie would tear the place down to get at it."

Lassie.

At home, Lassie's bedroom reflected his star status. It had a hi-fi set, an oversize bed, and paintings of Lassie on black velvet all around the walls. When he had to sleep away from home, Lassie also got star treatment — a hotel suite which Weatherwax was allowed to share.

Like Rin-Tin-Tin, Lassie finally retired. His place was taken over the years by five other Lassies, all descendants of the original star. Who says it hurts to have a famous name?

"The movie was a dog!" When you hear that about a movie with human actors, you know it means the film is bad. But if they say it about a flick starring a dog named Benji — you know it's good news.

Today Benji is the richest dog in the world. He gets $7,500 just for showing up on TV. He wears Brut cologne, travels first class, and dines on fat-free steak and vanilla ice cream.

They say behind every successful man, there's a woman. Well, behind every dog star there's an animal trainer. In the case of Benji, the man behind the dog is Frank Inn.

Frank owns an animal farm in California. From time to time, movie producers go there to audition four-legged performers. That's how Benji was "discovered."

The producer was Joe Camp, and he was looking for something special in the way of an animal actor.

"I want a dog that can really act," Camp told Frank Inn. "I need a dog with a point of view. I'm going to make a movie that will show a dog's-eye view of people."

Frank brought out big dogs, little dogs, cute dogs, fat dogs, thin dogs. Joe kept shaking his head. Then, as he was leaving, he spotted a small mutt with sad eyes and brown-and-white fur.

"You don't want that dog," Frank said. "He's too old."

It turned out that the dog was called Higgins, and he was about 13 years old. In human age terms, that would make him about 91. But if Higgins had been around

awhile, he had also piled up some acting credits. For seven years, he had been a star on the TV series *Petticoat Junction*. To keep his job, he had to learn a new trick every week.

Was Higgins ready for retirement, or for prime time? Joe Camp decided to find out. "Can he look intense?" Joe asked.

Higgins looked intense. No wonder. Behind Camp's back, Frank Inn was holding up a hunk of roast beef.

"I'm going to make this dog a star!" Camp predicted. And that's just what he did. First he changed Higgins' name to Benji. Then he starred him in a movie of the same name.

Benji (1973) was boffo — a super hit. For Higgins it was the whole star trip — talk shows, personal appearances coast-to-coast, jet lag.

But who needs that when you're 112? Three years later Benji-Higgins did retire for good. He couldn't care less about Joe Camp's plans for a sequel, *For the Love of Benji*.

Did this mean Camp was out of business? No, because Benji II, a chip off the old dog biscuit, was waiting in the wings. Like Benji, Benji II could kiss and hug at the lift of a director's eyebrow. And he was a real heartbreaker. The only difference was Benji II is a she.

Moviegoers probably didn't notice the difference, but Benji II is also somewhat bigger than Benji I. And she has a whole new bag of tricks. She can walk a tightrope, put quarters in a tollbooth basket, and take her fan mail out of the mailbox.

While Benji takes the bow-wows, Frank Inn takes a percentage of his dog stars' earnings. He deserves it, because he taught Benji I and II everything they know about acting. He also trained all the animals on *The Waltons*.

One of the most unusual talent hunts took place at Universal Studios in 1976. They needed a rooster to play Blarney, the mascot of a pirate ship in *The Buccaneer*.

Why isn't Blarney a household name today like Benji? Because the movie sank. Plans to put Blarney's claw-print in the cement in front of Mann's Chinese Theater in Hollywood were canceled.

Today Blarney is a has-been. The poultry market wouldn't even take him back.

Like many stars, Blarney was discovered by accident. He was in a coop on his way to a Hollywood poultry market. But the poultry truck overturned and Blarney escaped. He scuttled right to Universal, and a screen test.

His looks got Blarney the part. His bright red feathers and crimson comb photographed like a dream.

While the movie was filming in Mexico, nothing was too good for Blarney. He fell in love with a Mexican hen. The studio paid her expenses to Hollywood so she could be with Blarney when the shooting was over.

Have you ever wondered how animal stars are trained? Most Hollywood animal trainers agree with Rudd Weatherwax. "You praise them a lot," Weatherwax says. "You talk baby talk to them. They love it. They will do a lot for you if you show them you love them."

Benji.

Movie Animal Oddities

Tarzan meets elephant.

In the 1929 movie *Male and Female*, a scene called for a lion to jump on Gloria Swanson's back. Gloria didn't use a double. Instead, she slipped into a vest of loose canvas strips. The lion leaped, and the crew pulled the strips out from under the lion's claws one by one. "By the time the last strip was pulled away, the lion had relaxed and gotten used to me," Gloria recalls. Then the cameras rolled.

Puzzums, an alley cat, got parts in movies because he could cross his eyes and drink out of a baby bottle held between his paws.

In those old Tarzan movies starring Johnny Weismuller, the elephants had to wear false ears. That's because they were Indian elephants impersonating African elephants. Indian elephants are easier to train — but African elephants have bigger ears.

Animal trainer Ray Berwick specializes in bird actors for movies. He trained the birds for *The Birds* and the vultures for *The Andromeda Strain*. "Vultures are too shy to be anything but bit players," says Ray. "They have a bad reputation, but they don't deserve it. They're too timid to ever attack a living creature."

Ray also trained Fred, the cockatoo star of TV's *Baretta*. Fred was hatched in Hong Kong, and his real name is Lala. He started out speaking only Chinese, but Ray taught him pidgin English. Nothing is too good for Fred. He lives in a special cage equipped with a burglar alarm, and has a pet dog named Jeffrey. He even has double named Weird Harold who does his stunts and a stuffed cockatoo to be his stand-in.

A scene from *The Birds*.

Weird Tales from Hollywood

Superstition is big in show business. It's considered bad luck to whistle in dressing rooms or on soundstages. Comedian Stan Laurel changed his name because his real name — Stan Jefferson — had 13 letters. And some people believe that some movies are hexed.

For example, *The Omen*, a horror film, was bedeviled from start to finish. Star Gregory Peck and screenwriter David Seltzer took separate planes to London — but both planes were struck by lightning. When Harvey Bernhard, the producer, went to Rome, lightning hit Hadrian's Gate — just missing him. Stunt dogs hired for the film bit their trainers. A restaurant in which Gregory Peck was eating was bombed. Richard Donner, the director, was struck by a car. The special-effects director ended up in the hospital when his car crashed near the town of Omen in Holland. No wonder the cast and crew were a little nervous during the filming.

Lee Remick and Harvey Stephens in *The Omen*.

Maybe something didn't want these movies to be made, either:

• Typists working on the screenplay of *Salem's Lot* had to quit because of mysterious nosebleeds. *Salem's Lot* is about vampires.

• A mid-air collision over the Pacific in 1930 wiped out 10 members of the movie company of *Such Men Are Dangerous*.

• An unexplained fire wiped out the soundstages where *The Shining* was being made in February, 1979. *The Shining* is about a hotel with a curse on it.

David Soul and James Mason in *Salem's Lot*.

THE HAUNTED SOUNDSTAGE

For years rumors about a haunted soundstage have been floating around Hollywood. Some people say the soundstage is at Universal. Others say it's at 20th Century-Fox. And there are those who claim it was at Paramount, but it's been bulldozed down and paved over for a parking lot. When you ask studio heads about it, they claim they never heard of it. Can you blame them?

According to Hollywood old-timers, only two movies were ever started on this soundstage. Neither was finished there. One was a mystery set in London, but the studio fog machines never had to be used. The lenses on the cameras kept clouding over, all by themselves. The problem cleared up when they moved the filming to another soundstage.

The other film was supposed to take place in ancient Rome. Studio carpenters built a Roman temple there. Several marble columns were imported from Italy to be used in the scene. Each column was set in a special cement base. Yet when cast and crew reported for work, the

On the right is the mysterious Karl Dane.

columns were found lying on their sides. They had been lifted neatly out of their bases, as if by a giant. It took a full day's work to get the columns back in place again. At night, the soundstage was padlocked, and patrolled by guards with dogs. Yet the next morning, the columns were once more lying on the floor.

The best should be saved for last, so here goes. The Roman epic moved elsewhere, and the columns went with it. The soundstage stood empty for a time. Then one day it was used for a screen test.

The actor being tested was nervous. "I need somebody to bounce these lines off," he complained. "I can't put anything into what I'm saying if I just talk to the camera."

The director looked around. He saw a tall, hulking man with a heavily-lined face standing in the shadows out of camera range. "Would you mind coming over here for a few minutes?" he asked the man.

The man strode over. When asked if he would do the test with the actor, he nodded. When the test was over, he left.

That evening the director and an assistant watched the test in the projection room. When the big man's face flashed on screen, the director sat up straight. "Who is that guy?" he said. "I've seen him somewhere before. He's got a terrific face. Maybe we ought to set up a test for him."

The assistant ordered the test to be run through again. Then he shook his head. "No sense in setting up a test for him. That face belongs to Karl Dane. He died in 1934."

"You're crazy!" the director exclaimed. But everyone who saw the test agreed with the assistant. The face of the big man was indeed that of Karl Dane — or somebody who looked enough like him to be his twin.

Who was Karl Dane? He was a popular actor in the silent films of the 1920's. Sometimes he played the "heavy," sometimes the good-hearted fellow with more muscles than brains. He had starring roles in *The Big Parade* and *The Big House*. But as his career went downhill, so did his spirits. On April 15, 1934, he killed himself.

Was the man in the screen test Dane's ghost? Or was he just a Dane look-alike who happened to wander onto the haunted soundstage? No one knows. What we do know is that this mystery man never showed up again. He didn't even try to collect a day's pay for his services. And in Hollywood, they say you would *have* to be dead to let that happen.

The Dynamite Kids' Movie Quiz

Sure, you know all the important stuff about movies. But how about movie trivia — weird facts that are fun to tuck away in your head and amaze your friends with later? If that's the kind of movie fan you are, have we got a quiz for you! And here it is! If you can answer all the questions correctly without peeking at the answers first, maybe you should have written this book.

Who went ape when he grew up?

1. In the movie *Abbott and Costello Go to Mars,* where did they really go?
(A) The moon; (B) Cincinnati; (C) Venus; (D) NASA headquarters in Houston.

2. Which star was in the *Our Gang* comedies as a child?
(A) Robert Redford; (B) Christopher Reeve; (C) Robert Blake; (D) Mark Hamill.

3. Before *Star Wars,* director George Lucas made another science-fiction film. Which one of the following was it?
(A) *This Island Earth;* (B) *THX-1138;* (C) *Planet of the Apes;* (D) *Not of This World.*

4. Which of the following actors played *Superman* in movie serials?
(A) Kirk Alyn; (B) Bruce Cabot; (C) Buster Crabbe; (D) George Reeves.

5. In *Jonathan Livingston Seagull,* Jonathan's voice was dubbed by:
(A) James Franciscus; (B) Hal Holbrook; (C) Charlton Heston; (D) Richard Chamberlain.

6. Godzilla fans, pick out the monster that your hero *hasn't* done battle with in his many films.
(A) Ebirah; (B) Eegah; (C) Yog; (D) Hedorah.

7. What is the real name of the star who played the great white shark in *Jaws?*
(A) Orca; (B) Namu; (C) Bruce; (D) Flipper.

Was Hamill in *Our Gang*?

The man's named Gene — what's the horse called?

8. Ricky Schroeder, kid star of *The Champ*, began his career before the camera doing commercials for:
(A) diapers; (B) baby foods; (C) toys; (D) insurance.

9. Which of the following began his career as Elizabeth Taylor's co-star in 1943, and went ape in four science- fiction movies when he grew up?
(A) Mickey Rooney; (B) Dean Stockwell; (C) John Travolta; (D) Roddy McDowell.

10. Which child star was turned down for a part in the *Our Gang* comedies?
(A) Margaret O'Brien; (B) Deanna Durbin; (C) Jackie Coogan; (D) Shirley Temple.

11. What's a cowboy actor without his horse? In those old-time Westerns, horse and rider were co-stars. But who went with which? The cowboy stars' names are in Column A, and the horses' names are in Column B. Can you match them up?

A		B	
I.	WILLIAM S. HART	a.	Tony
II.	KEN MAYNARD	b.	Silver
III.	TOM MIX	c.	Champion
IV.	BUCK JONES	d.	Trigger
V.	GENE AUTRY	e.	Tarzan
VI.	ROY ROGERS	f.	Fritz

Think about it. How many movies can you see over and over? How many films look as good the third or fourth time around as they did the first time you saw them? Everybody has his or her own personal list of all-time movie greats, and here's ours. You may not agree with all our choices, but there are bound to be some on this list that will look as good to you time after time as they do to us.

58
Great
Dynamite Movies

THE DYNAMITE KIDS'
GUIDE TO THE MOVIES RATING SYSTEM

Each of the movies below has been subjected to our *Dynamite* bureau of standards. And we have found them all to be A-1 terrific. But to make things a little easier for you, we've come up with our system of symbols that tell you at a glance what to expect from each of these films.

KEY

1 smile — This film is really funny.

2 smiles — This film is so funny you might fall out of your chair.

3 smiles — Danger! This film is so funny you could laugh yourself sick!

1 tear — This film is really sad.

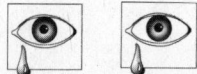

2 tears — This film is so sad, you'll need two handkerchiefs.

3 tears — This film is so sad, we can't even talk about it — boo hoo.

1 stick of Dynamite — This film is really exciting!

2 sticks of Dynamite — This film has so much action it could blow you out of your chair.

1 bat — This film is really scary.

2 bats — This film is so scary you'd better not see it when you're alone!

THE ABSENT-MINDED PROFESSOR
(Disney 1961)

It doesn't hurt to be absent-minded when you can invent something called *flubber,* as Fred MacMurray does in this wacky comedy. Flubber is a kind of rubber that pays no attention to the laws of gravity. Basketball players with flubber on their sneakers can leap to the stratosphere. A car with tires made of flubber can get a rise out of traffic. This film is a flight of fancy that's bound to tickle yours.

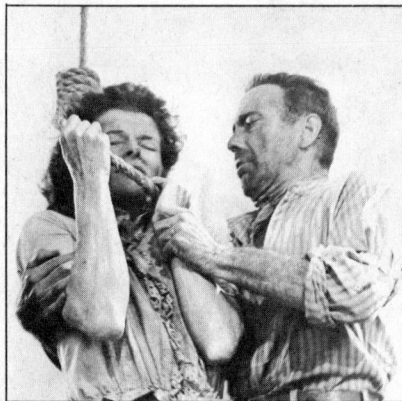

THE AFRICAN QUEEN
(United Artists 1952)

Humphrey Bogart and Katharine Hepburn go rolling down the river in a leaky steamboat. But the action is watertight in this adventure thriller set in Africa during World War I. Kate plays a prim missionary. Bogie plays a diamond-in-the-rough skipper. They're both on the run from German troops, and the ending is really a blast!

AMERICAN GRAFFITI
(Universal 1973)

Director George Lucas's really boss movie about being a teenager in 1962. The "graffiti" of the title includes sock hops, drag races, ducktail haircuts for the boys, ponytails for the girls. Then there are songs of the time such as "Teen Angel" and "The Great Pretender," all woven together by the talk of Wolfman Jack. As Wolfman says, "Awwright, Baay-Haaay-Baay, gotta oldie for you!" It's an oldie that will always be new because of great characters: John Milner (Paul Le Mat); Terry the Toad (Charles Martin Smith); sweethearts Steve and Laurie (Ron Howard and Cindy Williams); Curt (Richard Dreyfuss); and Laurie (Candy Clarke).

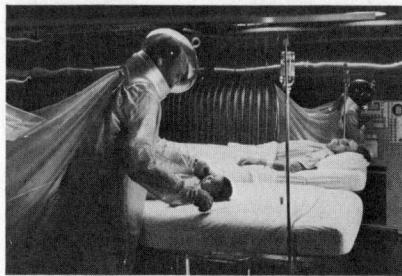

THE ANDROMEDA STRAIN
(Universal 1971)

Adapted from Michael Crichton's best-selling book of the same name, this science-fiction movie is a real spine-chiller. A U.S. space satellite falls back to Earth near a little New Mexico town. Hitchhiking on the satellite is an alien virus that kills on contact. A group of scientists fight the virus in an underground lab. If they can't come up with a cure fast, the lab will self-destruct. What happens next makes for a close encounter that's almost too close for comfort!

BAD DAY AT BLACK ROCK
(MGM 1954)

When a stranger (Spencer Tracy) comes to a Western town called Black Rock, trouble comes too. The stranger is there to bring a Japanese farmer the medal his dead son won in World War II. But the farmer has vanished and the townsfolk are pretty surly. There's a tough message about race prejudice, and lots of lean, mean action. A straight-shooter.

BEAUTY AND THE BEAST
(French Film 1946)

It's magic time, everybody! Eye-popping camera tricks and special effects turn this old fairy tale into a dreamlike fantasy for all ages. When Beauty (Josette Day) goes to the Beast's castle to save her father's life, she finds herself in a place where the lighting fixtures are living arms and a magic glove pulls her through walls. Like the castle, the whole movie is a spellbinder.

THE BIRDS (Universal 1963)

Birds are our fine-feathered friends, right? Wrong! Not in this Alfred Hitchcock scare-a-rama. For no special reason, birds go berserk in a California coastal town. There's no hiding place anywhere, so don't bother crawling under the seat.

BORN FREE (Columbia 1966)

She's blonde, beautiful, and weighs 400 pounds. She's Elsa, the lioness, the heroine of one of the best animal movies ever made. It tells the strange but true story of the Adamsons, a real-life couple who raise a lion cub and then give her back to the wilderness. It sounds easy, but how do you tell an oversized house pet that she's going to have to kill her own food and sleep out in the wilds?

BUGSY MALONE (Paramount 1976)

Remember those old-time gangster flicks with tough-talking hoodlums and shot-full-of-holes plots? Well, here's a gangster movie spoof with an all-kid cast and music by Paul Williams. Humphrey Bogart or Jimmy Cagney never starred in a more thrilling opening scene, either. Picture it — a rainy night in New York, 1928. Hoodlum Roxy Robinson is on the lam from rival mobsters. But they find him, aim their Splurge guns — and down goes Roxy under a barrage of whipped cream! Add Bugsy's (Scott Baio) romance with Blousey Brown (Florrie Dagger), and the torchy singing of Talulah (Jodie Foster) — and you've got a movie that's a killer!

CHARGE OF THE LIGHT BRIGADE (United Artists 1968)

"Was there a man dismayed?" wrote Alfred Lord Tennyson in his poem *The Charge of the Light Brigade.* If there wasn't, those British cavalrymen just didn't know what was happening. Using cartoons and live action, this movie re-creates one of history's loonier moments. It happened during the Battle of Balaclava, during the Crimean War (1853-56). Stupid and vain generals goofed, and sent 620 soldiers on horseback riding straight at Russian cannons. Only 190 of the British riders survived. This isn't a Hollywood battle spectacle. It's about people who tried and died and made a difference. David Hemmings is terrific as Captain Nolan. And after you see what Lord Raglan and Lord Cardigan were really like, you may never wear a sweater again.

CLOSE ENCOUNTERS OF THE THIRD KIND (Columbia 1977)

Every year, people all over the world claim they have had "close encounters" with UFOs (Unidentified Flying Objects). What are UFOs? This stunner of a movie comes up with a possible answer. Richard Dreyfuss plays a man whose life is changed by a "close encounter." It leads him to a mystery mountain and a mind-blowing solution. Wait until you see those UFOs touch down in a blaze of glory! Even if you think UFOs are nonsense, *Close Encounters* will make you want to believe.

CONRACK (20th Century-Fox 1973)

Can one person change the lives of others? Pat Conroy (Jon Voight) tried when he went to Yamacraw Island to teach some kids who didn't even know they were in the 20th century. Conroy (the kids call him "Conrack") tunes them into the here and now, and shows them how much fun learning can be. His methods get him fired, but he leaves the students with something they didn't have before — a sense of their own worth.

DAY OF THE DOLPHIN
(Allied Artists 1974)

Something fishy is going on in the lab of Dr. Terrell (George C. Scott). The "Something" looks like a fish, swims like a fish, and talks like Donald Duck. But it's not a fish. It's a dolphin named Alpha, and Dr. Terrell has taught it to speak English. When word of Alpha's talent gets out, some bad guys kidnap him and his mate, Beta. Their plan: To turn the dolphins into guided missiles. The message for dolphins is plain — button your lips and stay away from people! 👁️ 👁️ 🧨 🧨

DIARY OF ANNE FRANK
(20th Century-Fox 1959)

If you go to movies to forget the troubles of the world, this one's not for you. It's taken from the diary of a young Jewish girl who died in a Nazi concentration camp during World War II. It tells of the years when she and her family hid from German troops in the attic of an Amsterdam house. In this small space, young Anne grew into her teens, and then the hiding place was discovered. She died at 17, but there was no way of killing the spirit that shines through the diary she kept. The movie is tough viewing, but worth watching — and as hard to forget as Anne herself. 👁️ 👁️ 👁️

ENDLESS SUMMER
(Bruce Brown 1966)

To thousands of young people, surfing is *the* sport, and Bruce Brown is the "Fellini of the foam." Brown is a surfer himself. He has also spent years filming other surfers. This is a film he made with two other "hot doggers." In it, the three tote their surfboards to the beaches of Hawaii, Senegal, Ghana, Nigeria, Australia, New Zealand, and Tahiti. They prove that the sun need never set on a dedicated surfer. This movie will make you want to grab a board and head for the heavies, even if you don't live near the water!

FABULOUS WORLD OF JULES VERNE (Warner Bros. 1961)

Back in the late 1880's, Jules Verne was writing science fiction about machinery that hadn't been invented yet. Submarines, spacecraft, airplanes, and moon rockets were just a few of the things he put in his books. This film is based on his story *The Deadly Invention,* and it's about a cannon which fires atomic missiles. An extra added attraction is that many of the scenes start out looking like old engravings of weird machinery and stiff people. Then the machinery starts to hum, the pictures come to life — and that's entertainment, fans! 🧨

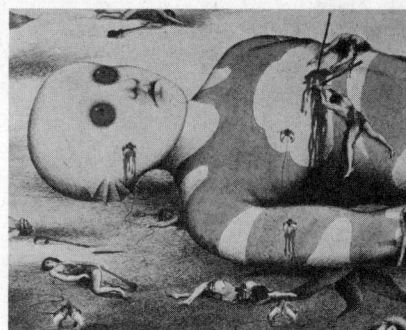

FANTASTIC PLANET
(New World 1972)

Walt Disney it's not, but a super science-fiction cartoon it is! It all takes place on the planet Ygam, home of the giant blue Draags and the tiny Oms. The Draags are androids who spend most of their time meditating. The Oms are humans, brought from Earth to serve as slaves and pets. Things look up for the Oms when Terr, a human child, is adopted by a Draag girl — and grows up to steal the secret of Draag power for his own people. Result: revolution — and an amazing discovery about the Draags. 🧨 ✈️

FANTASTIC VOYAGE
(20th Century-Fox 1966)

Most science-fiction shoots for outer space. This far-out thriller goes into the inner space of a human body. A top scientist is dying of a blood clot on his brain. A medical team is shrunk to microbe size, put into a mini-submarine, and injected into the patient's bloodstream. The team is armed with a laser beam to use on the blood clot — but they have to do it within 60 minutes. At the end of that time they will zoom back to normal size. And you think you have problems! ✈️ 🧨 🧨

FIDDLER ON THE ROOF
(United Artists 1972)

The hero of this sparkling movie musical is a burly, middle-aged milkman named Tevye (Topol). He has a lame horse, five unmarried daughters, and a nagging wife. He also has a hard time because he's a Jew living in a village in Czarist Russia. But Tevye has a lot going for him — humor, courage, a loving heart — and Tradition. Tradition, he tells us, is what tells him who he is and how to stay alive when the going gets tough. This one is everything a movie musical should be.

GONE WITH THE WIND (MGM 1939)

If ever there was a solid-gold golden oldie, this is it. No wonder they keep re-releasing it! Set in Georgia during and after the Civil War, it grabs your attention with characters that are more alive than most real people. There's Scarlet O'Hara (Vivien Leigh) who loves Ashley Wilkes (Leslie Howard), but marries Rhett Butler (Clark Gable). You can bet they won't try to make a new movie version of this one.

THE GUNS OF NAVARONE
(Columbia 1961)

Want to set the old pulses racing? Try this action-adventure epic on for size. It takes place in 1941, during World War II. Hundreds of British soldiers are trapped on a Greek island. British ships can't come to their aid because they'll be blown out of the water by the German-controlled guns of Navarone. Six men are picked to put the guns out of action on a suicide mission. The leader is an expert mountain climber (Gregory Peck). Does he lead his men to victory? Do movie guns shoot blanks?

FORBIDDEN PLANET (MGM 1956)

One of the all-time science-fiction greats! The crew of a spaceship from Earth lands on Altair, a desert planet with a green sky. There seem to be only three inhabitants — a scientist named Dr. Morbius, his pretty daughter, and their robot servant, Robby. But there's something evil loose on the planet that leaves footprints and dead crewmen around. When this Something becomes visible, you'll wish it hadn't! Guess where they got the plot for this one. Give up? It's a space-age version of William Shakespeare's play, *The Tempest.*

GREASE (Paramount 1978)

The class of '56 will never forget Rydell High. What a blast! The teachers were all comedians. The students were all groovy, especially Danny (John Travolta) and Sandy (Olivia Newton-John). At Rydell they don't do boring things like studying. Instead they major in dating, auto repair, drag racing, and getting ready for the big nationally televised Danceoff. Places like Rydell don't exist in real life, but lucky for all fun-loving viewers, it's here and now in this movie spoof of the 1950's. It's a super musical about the way it wasn't.

HAWAII (United Artists 1966)

For those who think movies about Hawaii are only about surfing and grass skirts, this is something completely different. It's about the first American missionaries who left Massachusetts in 1820 to bring Christianity to the Hawaiian Islands. There are good missionaries who work to help the Hawaiian people — and there's Abner Hale (Max von Sydow) who means well but is the biggest downer you ever saw. Abner not only makes the Hawaiians unhappy, he also ruins his wife's (Julie Andrews) life. The scenery is pretty, but the story is grim. The acting is terrific, especially the performance given by a non-singing Julie Andrews.

THE HAUNTING (MGM 1963)

What's that? You say you don't scare easily? Then you'll find this movie a real scream. A professional ghost hunter (Richard Johnson) zeroes in on a genuine haunted house. To really stir up the ghosts, he brings along two women who have had psychic experiences. The ghosts get stirred, the cast gets scared, and so will you. If you need inspiration for nightmares, don't miss this one. 🦇🦇

HEAVEN CAN WAIT (Paramount 1978)

Heavenly stuff. Joe Pendleton (Warren Beatty) is a quarterback for the Los Angeles Rams. His big ambition is to make it to the Super Bowl. But the dream and Joe both die on a Los Angeles freeway. But wait! It seems Joe shouldn't have died. An overeager angel (Buck Henry) jumped the gun and hauled Joe to heaven before his time. So Joe gets another chance at life — in the body of a millionaire marked for murder. There's lots more, all of it guaranteed to show how lively death can be. 👁️👁️👁️

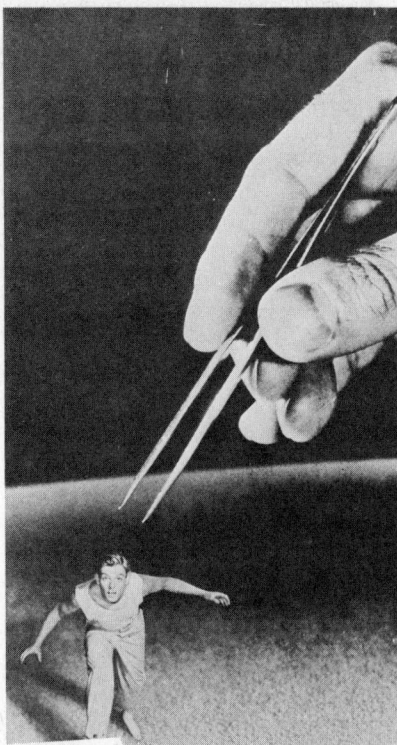

THE INCREDIBLE SHRINKING MAN (Universal 1957)

A movie to make Randy Newman take back what he wrote about short people. A scientist gets caught in an atomic cloud and starts shrinking. Day by day, in every way, he gets smaller and smaller. When he dwindles down to doll size and has to fight off the family cat, his wife gives up and leaves. But the poor fellow never stops shrinking. Soon he's out of sight and so is the film. 👁️🔪

THE INNOCENTS (20th Century-Fox 1961)

More ghastly ghostly goings-on. A governess (Deborah Kerr) is hired to look after two young children who may (or may not) be haunted by ghosts. Before long the governess is seeing ghosts, too. If this doesn't make you jump, maybe you ought to have your pulse taken. 🦇🦇

JAWS (Universal 1975)

Just when you thought it was safe to go to the movies, along came *Jaws* — the heartwarming story of a great white shark with a great big appetite. Come with us now to the town of Amity Island. A shark is gobbling up local swimmers right and left. Since Amity makes its living from summer tourists, something will have to be done about the shark. But whoever does that something would have to be crazy. Fortunately, there are three crazy people in town — the police chief, a scientist who specializes in fish, and a lunatic fisherman. If you hear a lot of screaming during this film, it will probably be you! 🦇🦇

THE JUNGLE BOOK (Walt Disney 1967)

Once upon a time there was a boy in India who was adopted by wolves. His name was Mowgli, and his adventures are part of one of the best books Rudyard Kipling ever wrote. They are also the inspiration for this terrific full-length animated cartoon. It shows how Mowgli grew up loving wolf-life, but knowing he would have to leave the jungle and learn to live with humans. You can't blame him for wanting to hang out with the animals forever. Except for Shere Khan, the tiger, they are friendly, witty, and fun. How many humans do you know that fit that description? 👁️

KES (United Artists 1969)

Billy (David Bradley) is a 14-year-old loner, living a glum life in a town in the north of England. His mother shuns him, his older brother bullies him. He has nowhere to go but up when he finds a wild kestrel (a small breed of hawk). He names the bird "Kes," and begins to train and tame it. For the first time, he has something to love — and to lose. This isn't a happy movie, but it has a lot to say.

LAWRENCE OF ARABIA
(Columbia 1962)

In 1935, a man named Ross was killed in a motorcycle accident in England. Ross turned out to be a mysterious figure who was known to the world as Lawrence of Arabia. To the Arabs, he was a hero because he led them to victory against the Turks. But what was Lawrence (or Ross) really all about? This big, sweeping movie gives us some of the answers. Peter O'Toole puts plenty of sand into Lawrence, and Omar Sharif plays a sheik to shriek over!

MOBY DICK (Warner Bros. 1956)

It's 1841, and Captain Ahab sets out from New Bedford on a whaling voyage. But the crew soon finds out that Ahab (Gregory Peck) is really out for just one whale — the great white one called Moby Dick. Years ago, Moby Dick bit off Ahab's leg — and Ahab isn't the kind to let bygones be bygones. This is a really mighty movie that will roll over you like a tidal wave. and leave you gasping.

KIM (MGM 1951)

A Kipling adventure goody about a half-caste orphan boy in India. Kim's mother was a Hindu, his father was a British soldier. Naturally Kim (Dean Stockwell) wants to do his bit for Queen (Victoria) and country. But even he gulps a bit when he's offered a chance to spy on Russian agents for the British. Paul Lukas almost steals the show as a mystery priest who befriends Kim. All the suspense and intrigue your nerves and fingernails can stand.

THE MIRACLE WORKER
(United Artists 1962)

A "must" movie for young people. It tells the story of one of the greatest real-life miracles of our time — how blind, mute, deaf Helen Keller came out of the dark of ignorance into the light of knowledge. At seven, Helen (Patty Duke) couldn't see, hear, or speak. Unable to communicate, she tormented her family with her wild rages. Could anyone teach this beast of a child to read, write, talk, and behave like a civilized human being? Annie Sullivan (Anne Bancroft) could and did. But first the Keller house became a battlefield in a war that ended up with two winners.

THE MUSIC MAN (Warner Bros. 1962)

A bouncing, breezy, zingy musical that could oompah you right out of your seat and start you marching. The time is 1912, the place is River City, Iowa. Enter "Professor" Harold Hill (Robert Preston). He fast-talks the townfolk into putting up money to start a boys' band. You know, to keep the kids out of the pool hall. Of course, Hill isn't really — or thinks that he isn't — going to use the money to buy band instruments. Lots of stomping dances and wall-banging songs. Also lots of brash, funny Robert Preston — of whom a lot is never too much.

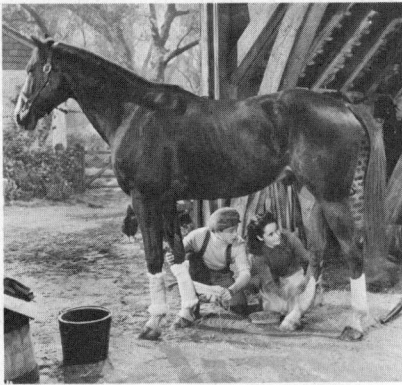

NATIONAL VELVET (MGM 1944)

Believe it or not, Elizabeth Taylor was once 12 years old. That's when she made this all-time favorite about a butcher's daughter named Velvet, and her horse Pye. Velvet's ambition is to ride in and win the British National. But in those days, only boys could be jockeys. A stableboy (Mickey Rooney) with a big heart helps Velvet train Pye — and maybe you can guess the rest. See it anyway. The plot may be corny, but it does grab you.

THE OUTSIDER (Universal 1962)

One of the most famous photos taken during World War II shows a small band of U.S. Marines raising the American flag on the Pacific island of Iwo Jima. One of those Marines was a Pima Indian named Ira Hayes (Tony Curtis). Because of the photo, Ira became a hero. But he couldn't handle his sudden fame. He pulled back from the good he might have done for his people and died an outcast. Tony Curtis turns in a top acting job that does the real Ira proud.

THE RED TENT (Paramount 1971)

In 1928, the Italian government got a far-out idea. Why not send some explorers to the North Pole in a blimp called the *Norge*? The expedition was commanded by General Nobile (Peter Finch), and it turned out to be a bummer. The *Norge* crashed, the crew was lost for weeks on an ice floe, and the great explorer Admundsen (Sean Connery) vanished while trying to find them. Nobile got blamed for everything. In this movie version of his misadventure, the ghosts of those who died put him on trial, and we get the story of what happened in flashbacks. Terrific stuff .

NIGHT OF THE HUNTER
(United Artists 1955)

A crazy backwoods preacher (Robert Mitchum) chases two young kids all over the landscape after he kills their mother. He thinks they're hiding their father's money. At times the movie is like a very bad dream. At other times it is as tough and hard-hitting as the old lady (Lillian Gish) who tries to help the kids out. Not for the fainthearted, but good does beat out evil in the end.

PLANET OF THE APES
(20th Century-Fox 1968)

Science fiction that doesn't monkey around. A spaceship from Earth crash-lands on an unknown world. Three astronaut survivors are taken prisoner by a race of intelligent apes. The humans soon learn that on this planet, people are regarded as inferior animals. Powerful stuff with a stinging ending that could be a warning for us all.

ROBINSON CRUSOE ON MARS
(Paramount 1964)

They can put a man on the moon. Why can't they send one to Mars? In this movie, astronaut Draper (Paul Mantee) gets to Mars. But his chances of getting back to Earth look dim. He's "shipwrecked," just as Robinson Crusoe was. Like Crusoe, Draper survives by using his wits and whatever is lying around. He even gets the Martian version of Crusoe's pal Friday, when UFOs arrive from another galaxy. A blast (off)!

ROCKY (United Artists 1977)

A knockout movie about a second-rate boxer (Sylvester Stallone) who gets a freaky chance to fight the world heavyweight champ, Apollo Creed (Carl Weathers). Not a Hollywood Cinderella story, but a serious look at a decent man who doesn't expect to win — just to do the best he can. Written by its star, this movie deserved the Academy Award and got it for "Best Picture" in 1977.

ROMEO AND JULIET
(Paramount 1968)

The world's most famous teenage lovers shine in this exciting movie version of Shakespeare's play. The time is the 15th century. The place is Verona, Italy, but the story is as modern as today! Teenagers Romeo (Leonard Whiting) and Juliet (Olivia Hussey) are in love, but their families are feuding. The kids elope and disaster follows. Bring plenty of tissues!

THE RUSSIANS ARE COMING, THE RUSSIANS ARE COMING
(United Artists 1966)

A Russian sub runs aground off Gloucester Island, Massachusetts. Hoping to beg, borrow, or steal a power boat big enough to pull the sub free, Lt. Rozanov (Alan Arkin) takes a landing party ashore. Rozanov's nine-man invasion turns out to a side-splitter. Every move the Russians make convinces the Gloucesterites that their island has been overrun by thousands of Russian troops. Panic buttons get pushed and common sense takes the day off. But don't worry. This is a *comedy* of errors — not a disaster movie.

SCROOGE (National General 1970)

What a Dickens of a character old Ebenezer Scrooge is! In this bouncy musical movie version of *A Christmas Carol*, Scrooge (Albert Finney) sings a lot of what he has to say. But the songs are catchy, so how can we mind? And the great old story is all there — cute little Tiny Tim, the four ghosts who spook Scrooge on Christmas Eve, the transformation of the old miser into the new kindly gift-giver. There's no humbug about this one.

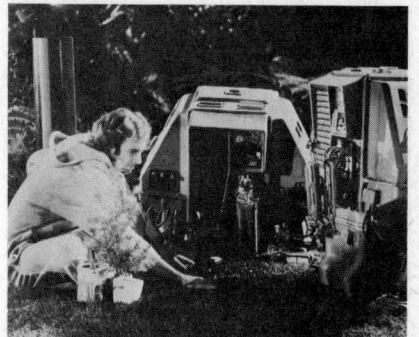

1776 (Columbia 1975)

And you thought history was dry stuff! Here we are with a musical that shows Ben Franklin as a Superstar; Thomas Jefferson as a Homesick Husband; John Adams as Mr. Unpopularity. And there's more, much more in this movie musical about the signing of the Declaration of Independence. *1776* isn't the kind of history you get out of books, but the songs, dances, and jokes make the facts easy to take.

SILENT RUNNING (Universal 1972)

In a future when Earth is paved over, where will all the forests go? Into outer space, says this science-fiction film. On space freighters, Earth's great forests grow under domes. But talking to trees gets scientist Lowell (Bruce Dern) into big trouble on the freighter *Valley Forge*. NASA decides to blow up the forests. Bruce decides to blow up the crew, and take the freighter to the rings of Saturn. With him go his robot friends, Huey and Dewey. These two have the greenest metal thumbs this side of Saturn!

SOUNDER (20th Century-Fox 1972)

This is truly a movie for everyone. It's the story of a poor black share-cropper (a farmer who works someone else's land) who steals food to feed his family. He is sent to prison, and his family tries to work the farm them-selves. When planting is done, the oldest son (Kevin Hooks) takes off with his dog Sounder to look for his father. The journey shows him how he can break out of the prison of poverty. An honest movie! 👁️👁️👁️

THE TIME MACHINE (MGM 1960)

This one is based on H.G. Wells' 1895 science-fiction stunner of a book. It tells of an inventor (Rod Taylor) who builds a machine that can travel to any year in the past or future. The inventor is looking for a time when the world is at peace, so he heads for the year 800,000 A.D. What a mistake! Only two kinds of people are left on Earth — the timid, laid-back Eloi and the savage Morlocks. Wells wrote a lot of books with sci-fi predictions that have come true. This one hasn't — yet! 💣💣

TO SIR WITH LOVE (Columbia 1967)

Rough stuff in a London school. Thackery (Sidney Poitier) is really an engineer. But because he is black, the only job open to him is teaching in a slum school. Faced with a class of teenage hoodlums, Thackery throws out the books and gives the kids a cram course in self-respect. 👁️👁️👁️

TRUE GRIT (Paramount 1969)

What's a nice kid like Mattie Ross (Kim Darby) doing in Yell County, Missouri? Trying to form a posse to hunt down her father's killer, badman Tom Chaney (Jeff Corey). In the time it takes to saddle up, Mattie ropes in two helpers. One is a crochety one-eyed lawman named Rooster Cogburn (John Wayne). The other is a Texas Ranger (Glen Campbell), who has his own reasons for lending Mattie his gunhand. You won't need a lot of other reasons for watching this humdinger. It's part old-time serial (see Mattie's fight for life in the snake pit!) and part spoof on old-time Westerns (see Rooster Cogburn's One-Man-Against-Three gunfight). 👁️👁️

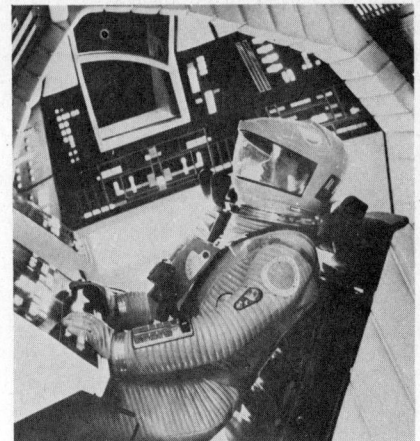

2001: A SPACE ODYSSEY (MGM 1968)

When pilots from Earth take to outer space, what will they find? According to this mind-blower, a strange slab floating out there and giving off signals. In trying to track the signals, a space-ship heads for Jupiter. By the time its gets there, the only crew members still alive are Bowman (Keir Dullea) and HAL, the ship's computer. HAL has more personality and emotions than Bowman. He (or It) is so busy thinking and feeling that his circuits overload and he freaks out. How would you like to be locked up in space with a crazy computer? Bowman doesn't like it, either. He jumps ship and heads for the wildest adventure anyone will ever have. 🛸💣💣

WALKABOUT
(20th Century-Fox 1971)

There are no ghosts in this movie, but it will haunt you. It's the story of a teenage girl (Jenny Agutter) and her younger brother who are stranded in the wilderness of Australia. A young Aborigine (an Australian tribesman) finds them. He becomes all the things they need — guide, playmate, and friend. But he can't keep them in the wilderness, and they can't take him to the city. This is a beautiful and unusual film. 👁️👁️💣

WAR OF THE WORLDS
(Paramount 1953)

From H.G. Wells, that wonderful guy who thought up *The Time Machine,* comes this tale of invaders from Mars. Stalking about on stilt legs, the Martian machines melt down resistance with their death rays. Will nothing stop them? The fade-out will make you glad medicine hasn't found a cure for the common cold.

WHISTLE DOWN THE WIND
(Pathe-America 1962)

When three motherless children on a lonely farm in northern England find a bearded stranger (Alan Bates) hiding in the barn, they decide that he is the Savior come back to Earth. They enlist the help of all the children in the neighborhood to hide the stranger from the grown-ups. This suits the stranger because he's a fugitive on the run from the police. However, the children's faith changes him. He's a different man when the police finally find him. Good performances by Bates, Hayley Mills, and 10-year-old Alan Barnes make you believe every frame.

WHITE DAWN (Paramount 1974)

In the 1880's, three New England sailors almost go down with their ship in Arctic waters. They are saved by a tribe of Eskimos. The Eskimos treat the sailors like family members until the tribe's luck (and the sailors') goes bad. A strange but true story based on a real-life disaster. In fact, many of the Eskimos in the film are descendants of those who rescued the sailors.

WIND AND THE LION
(United Artists 1975)

High-flying, high-adventure yarn about two real-life characters. One was Theodore Roosevelt (Brian Keith), 26th President of the U.S. The other was Raisuli (Sean Connery), a Berber chieftain of Algeria. Raisuli once kidnapped an American citizen and dared the President to do something about it. In this movie, the kidnapee is a young widow (Candice Bergen) with two children. You just know that T. Roosevelt isn't going to stand for that! Could the real happening have been this much fun?

Your Personal Top Ten

Okay, movie fans, now it's your turn. List your favorite, favorite films here. Then turn the page and see how many of your favorites made *The Dynamite Kids' Guide to the Movies* all-time great list.

1. _____
2. _____
3. _____
4. _____
5. _____
6. _____
7. _____
8. _____
9. _____
10. _____

What five movies
could you see once a week, and still want to
see the rest of your life?
Kids we polled agreed that these films
had the kind of appeal that just won't quit.
Here they are, fans —
the winners and all-time favorite flicks
of Dynamite Kids.

1. Star Wars

2. The Wizard of Oz

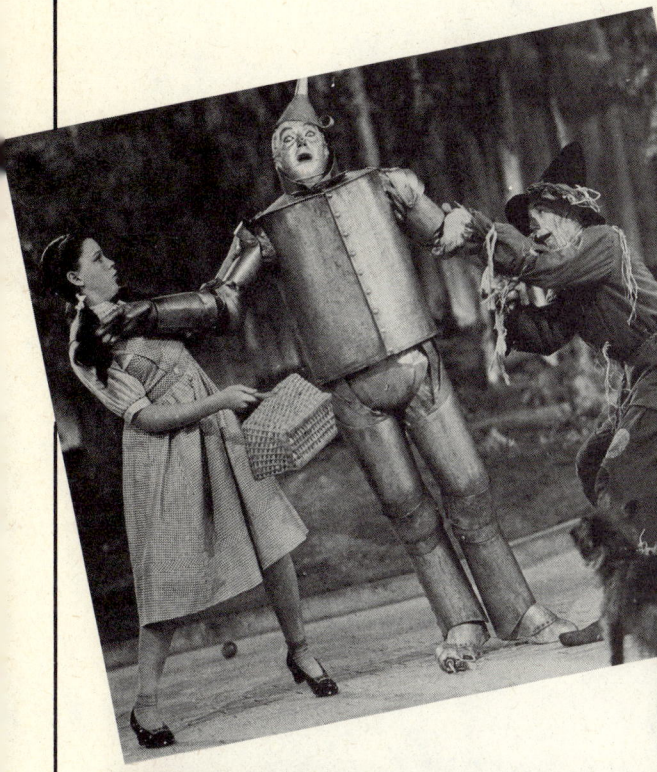

2. The Wizard of Oz

2. The Wizard of Oz

3. King Kong

4. Snow White

5. Frankenstein

Bibliography

Annan, David. *Movie Fantastic*. New York: Crown Publishers, Inc., 1974.

Barsam, Richard Meran. *In the Dark*. New York: Viking Press, Inc., 1977.

Edelson, Edward. *Great Kids of the Movies*. New York: Doubleday & Co., Inc., 1932.

Hagen, John Milton. *Holly-Would*. New Rochelle, NY: Arlington House Publishers, 1974.

Manchel, Frank. *Movies and How They Are Made*. Englewood Cliffs, NJ: Prentice-Hall, Inc., 1968.

— *When Movies Began to Speak*. Englewood Cliffs, NJ: Prentice-Hall, Inc., 1969.

Seuling, Barbara. *The Loudest Screen Kiss & Other Little-Known Facts About the Movies*. New York: Doubleday & Co., Inc., 1976.

Spehr, Paul C. *The Movies Begin*. Newark, NJ: Newark Museum Association, 1977.

Steinbrunner, Chris, and Burt Goldblatt. *Cinema of the Fantastic*. New York: Saturday Review Press, 1972.

Taylor, Theodore. *People Who Make Movies*. New York: Avon Books, 1967.

Wise, Arthur, and Derek Ware. *Stunting in the Cinema*. New York: St. Martin's Press, Inc., 1973.

PHOTO CREDITS

Practice Shelf-Hypnosis!

Cast a bright spell over your bookshelves and
turn your book collection from dull to Dynamite!
Collect the complete set of Dynamite Books.

Magic Wanda's Dynamite Magic Book
Count Morbida's Dynamite Puzzle Book
The Dynamite Party Book
The Dynamite Book of Top Secret Information
The Dynamite Monster Hall of Fame
The Dynamite Book of Bummers
The Officially Official Dynamite Club Handbook
The Dynamite Year-Round Catalog of Hot Stuff
The Dynamite People Book
Count Morbida's Fang-tastic Activity Book
Gotcha! The Dynamite Book of Sneaky Tricks,
Silly Jokes, and Harmless Pranks To Play On Your Friends
A Laugh and a Half: The Dynamite Book of Funny Stuff
The Dynamite 3-D Poster Book
The Dynamite Do-It-Yourself Pen Pal Kit
Good Vibrations: Straight Talk and Solid Advice for Kids
The Dynamite Animal Hall of Fame
The Dynamite Kids' Guide to the Movies
Dynamite's Funny Book of the Sad Facts of Life
The Dynamite Book of Ghosts and Haunted Houses
Count Morbida's Monster Quiz Book

U U A Q R R M M I I E E A A

U A Q R R M M I I E E A A

A V R R N N C J F F B B

V R R N N J F F B B

W S S O O J G G B B

W S S O O K G G C

X S S O O K H H C

X T O O L H H D

Y T P P L C C D

Y T P P L C C D

Z